The Mushroom Tapes

HELEN GARNER writes novels, stories, screenplays and works of non-fiction. She is the winner of the Melbourne Prize for Literature, the Windham–Campbell Prize for Non-fiction, the Australia Council Award for Lifetime Achievement in Literature and the Australian Society of Authors Medal. Her books include *Monkey Grip*, *The Children's Bach*, *The First Stone*, *Joe Cinque's Consolation*, *The Spare Room*, *This House of Grief*, *The Season* and *How to End a Story: Collected Diaries*.

CHLOE HOOPER is acclaimed for her compelling narratives in both fiction and non-fiction. She is the author of *A Child's Book of True Crime*, shortlisted for the Orange Prize for Literature, the multi-award-winning *The Tall Man: Death and Life on Palm Island*, *The Arsonist: A Mind on Fire* and *Bedtime Story*. She has won three Walkley awards.

SARAH KRASNOSTEIN is the bestselling author of *The Trauma Cleaner* and *The Believer*. Her prizes include the Victorian Prize for Literature and Walkley awards for both long-form feature writing and arts criticism. She holds a doctorate in criminal law and is admitted to practise law in New York and Victoria.

The Mushroom Tapes

Conversations on a triple murder trial

Helen Garner

Chloe Hooper

Sarah Krasnostein

TEXT PUBLISHING MELBOURNE AUSTRALIA

The Text Publishing Company acknowledges the Traditional Owners of the country on which we work, the Wurundjeri People of the Kulin Nation, and pays respect to their Elders past and present.

textpublishing.com.au

The Text Publishing Company
Wurundjeri Country, Level 6, Royal Bank Chambers, 287 Collins Street,
Melbourne Vic 3000 Australia

Copyright © Helen Garner, Chloe Hooper, Sarah Krasnostein 2025

The moral rights of Helen Garner, Chloe Hooper and Sarah Krasnostein to be identified as the authors of this work have been asserted.

All rights reserved. Without limiting the rights under copyright above, no part of this publication shall be reproduced, stored in or introduced into a retrieval system, or transmitted in any form or by any means (electronic, mechanical, photocopying, recording or otherwise), without the prior permission of both the copyright owner and the publisher of this book.

First published by The Text Publishing Company, 2025

Cover design by W. H. Chong
Page design and typesetting by Imogen Stubbs
Map by Simon Barnard
Epigraph from 'Emerging' by Pablo Neruda, translated from the Spanish by Alistair Reid for the *Paris Review*, Issue 57, 1974; originally published as 'Vamos saliendo' in Neruda, Pablo, *Estravagario*, Editorial Losada, Buenos Aires, 1958; with permission from Agencia Literaria Carmen Balcells, Barcelona
Quotation on pages 102–03 from Sheldrake, Merlin, *Entangled Life*, Vintage, Penguin Random House UK, London, 2021
Quotation on page 68 from Walls, Raymond A., *Five Fighting Shires: Korumburra 1891–1994*, Korumburra, 2008
Images on page 234 by Jean-Martin Charcot from *Iconographie photographique de la Salpêtrière*, Progrès Medical, Paris, 1880

Printed and bound in Australia by Griffin Press, a member of the Opus Group. The Opus Group is ISO/NZS 14001:2004 Environmental Management System certified.

ISBN: 9781923058750 (paperback)
ISBN: 9781923059603 (ebook)

A catalogue record for this book is available from the National Library of Australia.

The paper this book is printed on is certified against the Forest Stewardship Council® Standards. Griffin Press, a member of the Opus Group, holds chain of custody certification SCS-COC-001185. FSC® promotes environmentally responsible, socially beneficial and economically viable management of the world's forests.

and that's how we are, forever falling
into the deep well of other beings…
nobody can rescue us from other people

PABLO NERUDA

CONTENTS

PART I	The Court	1
PART II	The Church and the House	43
PART III	The Death Cap	83
PART IV	The Victims	121
PART V	The Accused	169
PART VI	The Verdict	211
	Coda	237

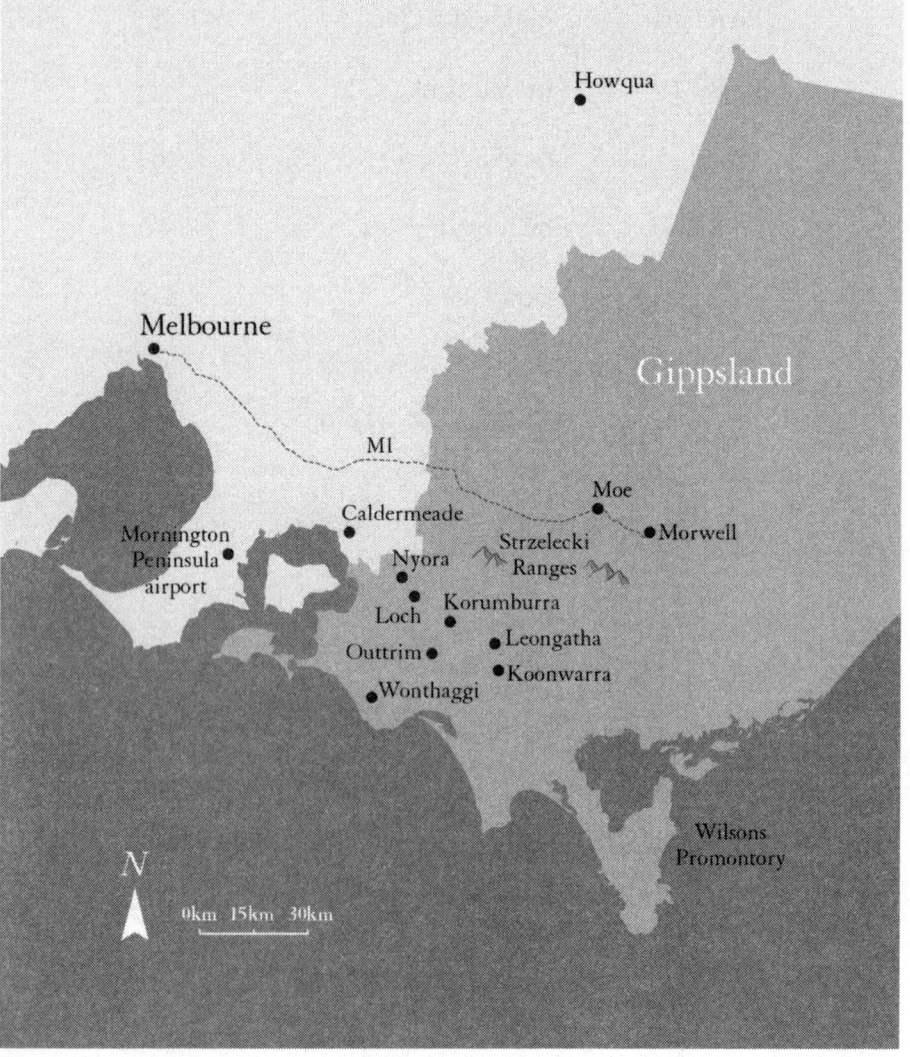

THE MUSHROOM TAPES

PART I

The Court

Monday, 5 May 2025

It starts and we are not even there. Everyone in the world is talking about it. People say to us, you must be going. No, we answer. No. No. No.

A woman is being tried for triple murder.

In the small town of Leongatha in South Gippsland, Victoria, the woman welcomed her estranged husband's parents, and his aunt and uncle, to lunch at her new house. She served the group, all of whom were devout Baptists, four individual beef Wellingtons, mashed potatoes and green beans. Within days, three of her guests were dead from death cap mushroom poisoning, and the fourth was in a coma.

Heads turn to watch the trial. We see them start to stir. Via a media audio-link we listen to the evidence of the woman's estranged husband. One wild domestic detail galvanises us: his dying aunt remembered that the guests ate off four grey plates, while the hostess served herself on an orange one.

On day five, we get in the car.

We head out of the city in a south-easterly direction.

Sarah Krasnostein is at the wheel, Helen Garner and Chloe Hooper are her passengers.

We've never travelled anywhere together before. We're writers and we're friends, but this morning we're almost shy of each other, not a hundred per cent sure how we're going to handle the day.

None of us wants to write about this. And none of us wants *not* to write about it.

Chloe: But if we were writing about it, what would our opening line be?

Helen: Here's one: *Breathes there a wife with soul so dead, who never to herself hath said, I'll kill them all and run away.* For some reason, it just shot into my head. I am shocked.

We check this is recording, just in case.

Sarah: Maybe we should locate ourselves. We're in my grey car and we have a two-hour drive ahead.

Chloe: The sun has just come up. There's a fish-scale sky and people are moving along the freeway to their jobs. Here's my opening line: *In every house, in every street along the M1, lives someone who knows the feeling of love gone wrong.*

Sarah: Well, I can't stop thinking about the orange plate.

Helen: While the other ones were grey.

Sarah: So my line is, *Twenty-two months after she served her lunch guests beef Wellington, the distinctive orange plate off which Erin Patterson had eaten came spinning out of the past like a frisbee and landed in front of the jury considering her murder charges.*

❖

Simon Patterson, the first witness for the prosecution, was questioned by Dr Nanette Rogers SC:

'You know the accused woman, Erin Patterson?'

'Yes, I do.'

'In what way do you know her?'

'I'm married to her.'

'Still married?'

His answer—'Correct'—is one that will puzzle us throughout the ten weeks of the trial. According to Simon's account from the witness stand, the marriage had begun well, with plenty of adventurous travel and outdoor life. They'd met while both were working in Melbourne, at Monash City Council, Simon as an engineer, Erin as an administrative officer in animal management. He was initially attracted to Erin, he said, for her intelligence and wit, and for her curiosity. Erin was raised an atheist but, while visiting his uncle's Korumburra church, she had a spiritual experience, and during their courtship began joining Simon in twice-weekly Bible classes. They married in June 2007. All her alleged victims were at the wedding—Simon's parents, Gail and Don Patterson, and his aunt and uncle, Heather and Ian Wilkinson.

Erin was not close to her own parents, but she inherited family money, quite a lot of it, and made generous, interest-free, no-contract loans to Simon's three siblings to help them buy homes. However, for reasons that were obscure, shortly after the birth of their first child in 2009, the marriage splintered into a series of separations, apparently initiated by Erin, and shaky reconciliations that Simon kept trying for. They had a second child in 2014. By 2015 Simon and Erin continued to consider themselves married, but lived in separate houses. Erin had also invited Simon to the family lunch on Saturday, 29 July 2023. He pulled out the night before, but a serve of poisoned beef Wellington was waiting for him, too.

Erin's defence barrister, Colin Mandy SC, claimed Erin loved her husband's family as her own. The Pattersons and Wilkinsons had always been kind and welcoming to her; their deaths, he said, had been a terrible accident.

❖

Heading along the freeway to Morwell, where the trial is being held, we compare notes.

Helen: Simon's a good witness, isn't he.

Sarah: He tells his part of the story steadily, with straightness.

Helen: Did you think he was crying? There were long pauses. Why did they keep parting? He said Erin had 'low esteem'. She was unhappy about her weight. I noticed an expression he used: 'I wanted to bring back right relationship between us.' That's a Christian term—people talk about getting into 'right relation with Jesus'. I wonder if it would wash with her, that sort of talk. Something isn't being said here.

Chloe: He told the court, 'She seemed a devoted mother, most of the time.'

Helen: The cliché about Baptists is that they're anti-pleasure. 'Why don't Baptists make love standing up? Because someone might think they're dancing.' But they've got a big reputation for basic decency. Being good, doing good, strong social conscience. Very strong on the Bible. Jesus is part of the fabric of your life. And you try, in my opinion quite reasonably, to live a Christian life. But that must entail a large amount of self-command and mutual criticism. Everybody's got their eye on you all the time.

Chloe: In a small town, everyone's got their eye on you already. But there's a mismatch between the modest, salt-of-the-earth relatives and Erin Patterson, who seems so operatic. Is that part of the public fascination? Why do you think this has struck such a chord?

Sarah: Female poisoner.

Helen: When you said *operatic*, I suddenly thought of *Medea*.

Chloe: It's *Medea* in reverse though. It's not her husband's children, she's alleged to have killed—it's his parents and elderly relatives.

Helen: I guess Medea in the sense that she's a *huge* figure. Her behaviour, if it's true, gives her operatic proportions.

Chloe: Why is the public fascinated by a female poisoner?

Sarah: It's archetypal. Adam and Eve and the apple. It's throughout myths and fairytales.

Chloe: These crime stories seem to work as modern folktales. We like it all the more if the characters are clearly good or bad, much as those old tales need a witch.

Helen: When I was splitting up with my husband, he said angrily to me, 'You think you're a good person!'

Chloe: Did you take that as an insult?

Helen: Oh, well, he certainly meant it as one. He'd probably had a gutful of my moral scruples. I flinched. It was an accusation of vanity and self-righteousness, or that's how I took it.

Chloe: Love gone wrong again.

Helen: But I don't get their relationship. A lot of thinking that goes on about murder is rather psychologically shallow. You know, people talk about motivation, which I always think is crude, like beating something mysterious with a hammer. But you know how people in crime stories always say, 'Follow the money'?

Erin's paternal grandmother, Ora Scutter, died in 2006 when Erin was thirty-two. Erin's share of the estate totalled about $2 million. The inheritance was disbursed over eight years, beginning in February 2007. Erin and Simon married soon after.

Helen: And was this when they gave money to his siblings as home loans? I'm wondering how that sat with her. You suddenly get access to two million bucks and you think, Cool—now I'm set up, I don't have to worry about the future. And then, somehow, because of your husband's belief—or your shared belief—in duty to family, it kind of leaks out sideways.

Chloe: I see it differently—it's a way of her controlling other people. The money meant that everyone was beholden to Erin because she'd enabled various parts of their lives. And perhaps her abrasive behaviour was normalised, or excused, because everyone was in her debt.

Sarah: Or maybe the family were, in her opinion, not appropriately grateful. Maybe there were slights, real or perceived, and Erin didn't get the respect or the love or inclusion she felt was her due.

Chloe: And she started to feel resentful.

Sarah: That's right. There's not a lot of data on female poisoners, but in what I've read about the typical profile there are strong wish-fulfillment fantasies. If you've got delusions about your own power or entitlement—if you expect more from relationships than what's reasonably attainable—where does all of that take you? Erin's intelligent. She was well-travelled. She had the money to build her dream home. There's a gap between grand expectations of life and marriage, and the damp reality of doing the school run in a country town, getting older, mingling with the same small church community—maybe you feel trapped.

We'd heard from the prosecution that in the year leading up to the lunch there had been ill feeling between the couple, which showed in a series of administrative slights. Simon had attracted Erin's ire by specifying his marital status as separated on a 2022 tax form. He, in turn, was upset when she claimed child support. Erin's mother died in 2019 and Erin received another multimillion-dollar inheritance. She owned various properties and there were disagreements about whose name should be on the titles.

We were trying to keep up with it all.

Sarah: The tax form, and then that conversation about child support, they seem to be a watershed moment, if that's how these things work. Maybe Erin felt cast out or used, or extreme rage or fear, over what he was doing behind her back.

Chloe: And, around this time, she was offended at having received a late invitation to Gail's seventieth birthday party.

Sarah: Then three weeks before the lunch Erin took the kids out of their school without consulting Simon and sent them to a different one. It was downhill from there.

❖

We come over the crest of a rise and see the Yallourn power station outside Moe, the last town before Morwell. We're now in brown-coal country and at the centre of the Latrobe Valley's industrial heartland. Morwell is on the edge of a mammoth abandoned coal pit, and it's one of the most socially disadvantaged places in the state.

Chloe: The Pattersons and Wilkinsons lived in Korumburra, near where my in-laws live. It's a very different part of Gippsland, on the other side of the Strzelecki Ranges. It's ten minutes down the road to Leongatha, where Erin held the lunch. Sarah, you're a lawyer, why has Erin decided to hold her trial in Morwell?

Sarah: A person has the right to be tried in the court closest to where they live or where the offending allegedly occurred. Maybe she's had legal advice that there are forensic advantages to having it in Morwell with a jury of locals instead of in the Melbourne Supreme Court. Or maybe this is the result of her own instructions. If that's the case, putting myself in her shoes, I reckon she chose Morwell for two reasons. One, I'm sensing she has a strong desire for control wherever she can exercise it, and this location would give her the advantage of making life harder for everyone involved in prosecuting her. Two, it's a smaller courtroom, which she perhaps thought would limit the number of people looking at her.

Should we talk about why we decided not to write about this case individually?

Helen: I love courts, and I love trials, and I miss that world terribly. I love watching the law trying to deal with people and how jagged and horrible and violent we are. You can feel the spirit of the law in a courtroom. But I'm getting old. I'm probably at the end of my working life. I haven't got the wherewithal to follow a big trial by myself. So I'm really glad you asked me to come with you.

Chloe: Well, I've covered, in book form, two crimes, a death in custody and a deliberately lit bushfire—actually, the fire was started very close to Morwell. For me, those crimes opened up deeper stories about Australia. With Erin Patterson, I can't quite read the layers under what appears to be primal violence. I think, too, in all crime stories, there's a limit to your appetite for sitting beside misery—the family's, the children's. I didn't know if I could manage it. I still don't. Working together, though, our eyes will go to different places. Maybe we can make something more than the sum of our parts.

The day the trial started, I texted Sarah, 'FOMO?' And she wrote back, 'JOMO'.

Sarah: That was the joy of not being there, of not being terrified to miss a detail you need later back at the desk. This case was on my radar. I did wander into the preliminary proceedings a few times.

Helen texted Sarah, asking if she was going to the trial. Chloe wrote to Helen: Do you want to work with us? Helen wrote back: I'm in.

In truth we don't exactly know what we are going to do with what is already an hour and a half of tape. Will it be a podcast or a book? But we're warming up to the conversation.

Sarah: I identify strongly with what Helen said about the spirit of the law. When the power of the state is working properly, there's something that's larger than its parts in a courtroom. There's the idea that we're trying to repair a rift in shared ethics. And there are so many little things, quiet details, that can reveal the human weight of the story. They're usually missed under the strain of trying to file, on a daily basis, the most salacious points of the story. If you're doing it right, you will carry these people and their pain for the rest of your life.

Helen: What's fascinating about crime is that there's a sort of membrane that separates people like us, ordinary people who don't murder, from someone who does. And I always want to look at the person whose foot has gone through that membrane, who has wrecked their own life by ending someone else's. But what you almost always see when you look at an accused person is a broken person. A person who has gone out there where none of us have let ourselves go, but where we all fantasise about going. Who hasn't thought, Oh, God, I'll kill that bastard? So I always have a weird kind of empathy for the person in the dock, and it comes and goes as the trial proceeds; it's not that I'm big-hearted or anything, it's just that I have this awful feeling—that could be me.

Sarah: It's never *not* a shock to me, that normal aspect. There's no sign over the dock that says *Evil*. The mundanity is always the most chilling discovery.

Helen: Basically what we're doing is bearing witness. And

you almost quoted Hannah Arendt's expression, a rent in the social fabric, as she called it. We're bearing witness to a rent in the social fabric and how the law is going to deal with it.

Sarah: After I finished law school, I was in the County Court to watch the sentencing of a guy for child-sex offending. It was totally bureaucratic, and I felt ashamed to even look at him. And then I thought, I'm going to look, and keep on looking when he sees me, because I'm the only one here bearing witness.

Chloe: But I guess the *Daily Mail* and the *Herald Sun* and a flotilla of other journos will also be in Morwell bearing witness. Is our bearing witness actually more high-minded or are we dressing up our own motives?

Sarah: I think there's a false assumption that any attention on this trial is inherently wrong. Not all attention is equal. I remember a reporter saying to me once, when we were waiting around for the verdict after a major trial, 'Ugh, we don't know if it'll be today, so I'll go to the pub and have a couple of drinks, and then they'll call the verdict, and I'll be drunk, and it will be harder to chase the family down the street—don't you hate that?' I have no experience along those lines.

People are forced by the rules of evidence to disclose things in public that they would probably not even admit to themselves. And you can do two things with that. You can digest it into content that people come to ogle out of schadenfreude, or you can say, 'Oh, God, I know that feeling. I haven't had that exact experience, but I know what shame is, and I know what rage is, and I know what it is to be isolated and desperate.'

Chloe: Here's the turn-off.

Sarah: I'm thinking about the room we're about to walk into. The sorrow it contains. *Medea* is an interesting comparison because, like this, it's a horror story.

Chloe: Simon's lack of comprehension and his enormous grief were very, very clear, listening to his voice.

Helen: Yes, those long silences and then at the end you'd hear him take a breath.

And yet I agree with you, Kras, that it's public. It's a rent in the social fabric and it's grievous and horrible, but I would hate to think I was just perving. There is that element, of course, but you hope that by the time you've got a certain degree of skill as a writer, you can become useful. I think it's useful work. These trials are excruciatingly painful. Your description of that journalist, going to drink at the pub—that's defence, isn't it, defence against the pain. The pain that you volunteer to witness.

Chloe: We're coming into Morwell. The town will have been transformed by the media pack. That's a story in itself, but I don't think we should turn back.

In Morwell's courtroom four there are only thirty public seats. We find they are mostly reserved for the Patterson and Wilkinson families, their church supporters and six balloted media representatives. The room is panelled in honey-coloured wood and is full of light, which streams in through a large picture window. Aboriginal artworks line the walls.

Due to its size, everyone is close together—and everyone is also close to Erin Patterson.

She sits in the dock at the back of the courtroom, flanked by two custody officers. She wears a taupe-coloured top. Her hair is long, dark and straight. Out of politesse, she smiles slightly if someone meets her eye, then moves her gaze. The woman who appeared on national news bulletins weeping flamboyantly for her dead relatives has disappeared. The gravity of the room has stripped away any layer of the ridiculous. The layout means Erin is now surveying the media and everyone else in the court.

We find spare seats in a row directly in front of her.

From our vantage point we can see Justice Christopher Beale sitting, at altitude, behind the bench, his clerk at a computer nearby.

The black-robed barristers sit before piles of folders at the long bar table in front of the bench. To the left is Erin's defence team, led by Colin Mandy SC, a man in his fifties with short, dark hair in a widow's peak, and a way of tilting his head and looking up from under his brow with a sombre, measuring expression. To the right, are the lawyers for the Crown, led by the fast-moving Dr Nanette Rogers SC. She has a habit of ruffling her grey, curly hair with an impatient two-handed movement.

To our right is the jury: fifteen people, randomly selected from the surrounding towns.

A man is ushered in and walks calmly to the witness box. It's Simon Patterson. Bald, with a flushed complexion, he is a dignified presence in a grey suit and white shirt. An Art Nouveau vine twists down his tie. He does not look in Erin's direction, and it is unclear what cord now connects husband and wife—whether it is love, hate, God or grief.

Simon had previously told the jury that Erin had invited him and his family to the Saturday lunch to discuss a health issue. At the last moment he had cancelled. On Sunday morning, he received a call from his father, Don: his parents were heading to hospital with dire gastric symptoms. Simon then called to check on his aunt and uncle. Unable to reach them by phone, he drove to the Wilkinsons' home. Ian and Heather were also in a terrible way, and he insisted on driving them to Leongatha Hospital. On the way, Heather mentioned the single orange plate and asked, 'Is Erin short of crockery?'

By Monday the four guests had been transferred to Melbourne's Austin Hospital for urgent treatment. Simon described his final conversations with his mother and father: Don said that, when the meal concluded, Erin told her guests she'd been diagnosed with cancer. She needed the family's advice on how to break this news to her children. Don, a former physics teacher, had always got along well with his daughter-in-law, who, like him, was a reader and intellectually curious. Simon said that as Don and Gail deteriorated in hospital they were worried for Erin's health.

Mandy put it to Simon that Erin had told her guests she suspected she might have cancer, not that she had a positive diagnosis.

'It is possible there's a flying teapot going around Mars,' Simon replied, 'but pretty unlikely.'

With his wife looking on from the dock, Simon closes his eyes, trying to breathe.

He rotates a slight degree very slowly on the chair, over and over.

He picks up a paper cup, sips, puts it down.

He had found it surprising, he says, that although he'd called his wife to inform her of the Pattersons' and the

Wilkinsons' conditions, she did not ask again after their health. Instead, she told Simon that she was feeling very unwell.

There's the hum of the split-system heater. The susurrus of lawyers and journalists typing out his words.

Colin Mandy, who can adjust the dynamics of his voice with a musician's rigour, asks Simon if he had contacted his parents the day after the lunch to ask about Erin's health?

Simon's smile is controlled: he can see the absurdity of this.

He says when Erin had invited him to this lunch, arranging it for a fortnight's time, he remembered feeling puzzled. If his wife had a serious medical issue, why was she waiting two weeks to tell them?

Behind us, Erin looks small and nervous in the dock. Now when we turn to glance at her, she flinches slightly.

The court adjourns at 1 pm for lunch.

Simon Patterson walks out of the courthouse into a blaze of photography and does not return for the remainder of the trial.

❖

By the time we leave the court, numerous camera crews and television journalists are standing idle. We pass them and find a cafe called Jay Dee's just across the road.

Chloe: It struck me that, rather than us observing Erin, she's observing all of us.

Sarah: Watching her requires fairly assertive turning of the head.

Chloe: I was thinking of what you said in the car. About how, actually, one *should* look at the accused. And so I did. She is a striking presence, isn't she. And slightly unexpected.

Sarah: I wasn't quite brazen enough to have a really good look. And she was very aware of being looked at.

Helen: She appears younger than she did in those photos taken before she was arrested. Her hair is longer and darker. My immediate thought was, She was once a good-looking girl.

Sarah: I don't find her unnerving, definitely not scary.

Chloe: Her gaze hit the side of her husband's face.

Sarah: I had no sense of her being in any way different from anyone I would encounter.

Chloe: I felt conscious of her, I had a tiny shiver on the back of my neck.

Helen: What about Simon's self-command. He's really got a grip on himself, hasn't he? But not in an awful way. To me, he's being very, very careful, and he will not be rushed. He's impressive, and he's likeable. He won't go along with something just to keep it rolling.

Sarah: But there's strong emotion just beneath the surface.

Chloe: His tone's even more astonishing when you think, this man has been in a coma.

Helen: *He* was in a coma! *What?* How did you hear that?

Chloe: I read about it in the *Daily Mail*. He wasn't expected to live. In 2022, a year before the lunch, he was hospitalised a few times and his family were called in more than once to say goodbye.

Helen: I'm not a subscriber…Oh hell, what else have I missed?

Chloe: There were three other charges against Erin for attempting to murder Simon, but for complex reasons they were discontinued on day one of this trial. Justice Beale instructed the jury to put them out of their minds.

Helen: I thought they must have just been rumours about her that the judge was hosing down.

Sarah: I think of Simon allegedly being poisoned as the ghost case here. In a courtroom, you're watching an artifice at the best of times. The legal story is always haunted by a whole chunk of reality that's excluded from the room by the rules of evidence. But here, the story of Simon's poisoning is running under everything that's being said.

Food is now being brought to us at our outdoor table.

Helen: The thing about female poisoners is it's the flip side of mothering. It's the most appalling betrayal of what women are supposed to be like. We're supposed to nourish and put in front of people food that brings life to them. This story is an inversion.

We read that Erin Trudi Scutter was born in 1974 to Heather Scutter, an academic and expert in children's literature, and Eitan 'Hugh' Scutter, a company director. She grew up in the middle-class, south-eastern suburbs of Melbourne with one sister, who later studied the fracture behaviour of volcanic glass. In 1992, Erin started a science degree at the University of Melbourne, then switched to accounting. She completed training, and worked for a time as an air-traffic controller.

Chloe: This is from a former air-traffic colleague of Erin's. Erin 'was regarded as something of a genius. She's very bright and much brighter than people might think. She managed to get guys wrapped around her little finger, although she was very unkempt.'

Sarah: Unkempt?

Chloe: You mightn't want her organising the skies, but it wasn't a school of deportment.

Sarah: I presume that in the past poison was a common way to get rid of an abusive husband or elderly relative for inheritance purposes.

Chloe: Or to make them sick enough to control them. Is there a Munchausen-by-proxy situation going on?

Helen: Well, Mandy raised this possibility when he listed the suite of other illnesses that she'd previously claimed to have.

Sarah: I'm looking it up. It's now called factitious disorder. It used to be known as Munchausen syndrome, where people feign a medical condition to elicit treatment or attention, or Munchausen-by-proxy, where they make others sick in order to play the caregiver.

Chloe: Poisoning your husband was once referred to as the 'Italian method'. In the seventeenth century, an Italian woman sold bottles of odourless poison called Aqua Tofana. It was marketed as healing water.

Helen: Women had to use a sneaky method—a man could seize a weapon and turn it against you.

Chloe: On Saturday night, at a party, I was talking to a beautiful woman who is married to a difficult man. There are frictions around the children, and she said, 'I feel when women give birth something else is born. The placenta may as well be resentment.'

Sarah: Oh my God.

Chloe: I had a conversation afterwards with my partner about how even in good relationships there are moments where love brushes very close to hate. And he agreed.

Rather too readily, I thought.

Sarah: When women kill, it's mostly for protective purposes, for themselves or their kids. That's where my mind went when I first read about this case. Someone like Heather Osland resorted to murder after years of the worst violence. We've had no indication there was anything like that here.

Chloe: No.

Sarah: And yet how swiftly that resentment—or whatever it was—escalated to such a cunning, premeditated plan. I mean, just the pastry alone. And then you get into the dehydrating.

Helen: What about her text message, when Simon begged off coming to lunch. What a guilt trip.

> Simon at 6.54 pm, Friday, 28 July 2023: Sorry, I feel too uncomfortable about coming to the lunch with you, Mum, Dad, Heather and Ian tomorrow, but I'm happy to talk about your health and implications of that at another time if you'd like to discuss on the phone. Just let me know.
>
> Erin at 6.59 pm, Friday, 28 July 2023: That's really disappointing. I've spent many hours this week preparing lunch for tomorrow which has been exhausting in light of the issues I'm facing and spent a small fortune on beef eye fillet to make beef Wellington, because I wanted it to be a special meal as I may not be able to host a lunch like this again for some time. It's important to me that you're

all there tomorrow and that I have the conversations that I need to have. I hope you'll change your mind. Your parents and Heather and Ian are coming at 12.30. I hope to see you there.

Helen: She might have already tried to kill him, and she probably had one last go in her, which was his serve of the beef Wellington, and then he fucked it up by not coming. Maybe she thought, Well, it's the church and your family that you've chosen over me the whole time: I'm going to go full revenge.

Sarah: Again, poison is a small thing. It is invisible and happens at a remove. It is Janus-faced. It's a coward's weapon.

Chloe: I think you *could* be brave and be a poisoner.

Sarah: I don't think you can. I mean, this is the debate: for the affirmative, can you be a brave poisoner?

Helen: Well, it depends who the victim is, of course. I mean, if it was some trashy dictator—

Sarah: Yeah, empty the Lucrezia Borgia ring into his McDonald's Coke, into his vodka—*dup, dup, dup.*

❖

Following the death of her mother in 2019, Erin used some

of her inheritance to buy a townhouse in Mount Waverley and a three-acre block in Leongatha, on which she and Simon planned to build a new home together.

Simon helped to hire the architect and builder, but he told the court he'd wondered 'whether she was using me for my expertise and contacts to build her house, or whether she genuinely thought this was, you know, a move towards living as a family again'.

Chloe: When Simon talked about designing the house he talked about the library, which didn't materialise.

Sarah: He said, 'There was supposed to be a library full of books.'

Chloe: Erin grew up as a reader. Her childhood home, they say, contained an extraordinary number of books.

Sarah: The sadness of building this library at the heart of the house that then becomes the 'computer room'. I'm struck by the odd ways distance and isolation figure in the story. When Erin asks Simon for help with a fallen tree, he writes back, 'I'm always your husband, no matter how we're doing.' And yet there was this gaping distance between them. Then there's the distance between who she was and how she presented to the Pattersons. How the fact of physical proximity doesn't necessarily mean that you truly know a person.

Marriage is a story that requires constant updating, because you have the idealisation of first love, and then living together, then having kids—

Chloe: And then you find out who you're actually married to, and you try to slowly fit the pictures together...

Sarah: ...and you're changing and they're changing. What does it mean to abide in a relationship? Well, it means having to adapt and, I suppose, to mourn constantly those old or outdated idealisations.

Chloe: Editing the story of who the person is you're married to.

Sarah: Or you delete it entirely and start again.

Chloe: That's the danger zone.

❖

When court sits again after lunch, the prosecutor, Nanette Rogers, tells the jury that much of Erin's socialising took place online. Using a number of different names, including 'ErinErinErin', Patterson joined such Facebook groups as 'Keep Keli Lane Behind Bars'. Here, a thousand or so members discussed the case of Keli Lane, a star water-polo player who was accused of hiding five pregnancies and later convicted of killing one of her babies. Other true crimes were discussed, but the group was riven by personal conflicts and Erin then joined a breakaway chat group of twenty to thirty people called The Ex–Keep Keli Lane Behind Bars group, or XKKLBB. A smaller chat group again then formed, consisting of Erin and four other women.

Three of them now testify one after another via video link.

Christine Hunt says that Erin shared that she and Simon had grown apart and were living separate lives. 'I understood that she was self-sufficient, although she had some concerns about him paying his share...he was very controlling. She'd used the word "coercive" at times and also that his family were very demanding and that she was really challenged by their demands.'

When asked how Erin painted Simon as a father, Hunt replies, 'Abusive through that kind of coercive control was the sense that we were given. Disagreed with her lots, in particular around some medical things. [Her] being an atheist and Simon being from a very strong Baptist background, she found that very challenging...in particular the decisions around things like divorce, separation, and particularly around the kids' education...She didn't like it.'

On cross-examination, Colin Mandy puts it to Hunt that while Erin had been an atheist in the past, at the time of their group chats she believed in God.

'I think she was two-sided on that,' says Hunt bluntly.

Daniela Barkley testifies that Erin shared details about her relationship with Simon. 'Just sometimes how sad she felt, about how he was just so religious and how it was so difficult, I don't know, to get along with him, I guess.'

'Did she post things about what she thought of Simon?'

'Just that he wasn't a very nice person.'

❖

Court ends at 4 pm. We're driving back to Melbourne now in the late afternoon sunlight.

Helen: If anybody wants a mandarin or a biscuit, just kindly scream out and I'll pass it over.

Chloe: There was a submission from Erin's barrister asking for Erin to be given pen and paper and a computer in her cell.

Sarah: To make notes for her lawyers. She is apparently a great researcher, 'a super sleuth' it was said.

Chloe: I had a strange feeling today that we'd entered a true-crime tale and it was unclear who the author was. As if Erin had left her online group to become the author of this.

Sarah: Think about all the other friendships that are now forming in Erin Patterson Facebook groups. It's like true-crime inception.

Chloe: Weirdly it felt less voyeuristic being there in court. We were just following this strange river that everybody, including Erin, was swimming in.

Sarah: The women in the chat group described talking about their kids and their marriages and the news and politics and cooking. The group was a social support for them. Perhaps it was Erin's only close friendship group.

Chloe: When they mentioned the Keli Lane case, I thought, Medea has entered the courtroom. We are back in women-and-motherhood territory.

Sarah: But, despite texting most days, sometimes all day, they wouldn't have known each other's voices, or even necessarily recognised each other's faces. They did cast a new light on Erin's marriage: her feeling that Simon privileged the church and his family over her and the kids.

Helen: The way he gives evidence on the stand—that controlled nature. He's very quiet and takes his time and at first I thought that was admirable. But you flip that over and if you're his wife you are arguing against a wall of reason and…well, actually, righteousness. Yeah. I started to feel that he could be an adamant kind of person.

Chloe: Simon has a media advisor with him in the courtroom. She came up to one of the journalists after the evidence that suggested he was controlling. The advisor was getting on the front foot. She told the journalist that she wanted people's email addresses. He may put out some sort of corrective to that evidence.

Helen: He wants to control the narrative and what people think of him.

Sarah: That's what a court case is, though—two partial narratives fighting it out.

The chat-group women's evidence included that Erin was 'a bit excited that she'd purchased a good dehydrator'. She posted photographs of mushrooms on kitchen scales being weighed and then on the trays of her new dehydrator. There were screenshots of Erin's comments to the group:

> Fun fact: dehydrator reduces mushroom mass by 90%.
> Do you think Woolies would mind if I brought it in and reduced them before buying?
> I've been hiding powdered mushrooms in everything. Mixed into chocolate brownies yesterday. Kids didn't have a clue.

Sarah: Oh, and Erin asked the group two weeks before the lunch whether anyone could give advice on cooking a beef Wellington. She checked in with the group about what cut of meat to use. She asked for tips about keeping the pastry moist.

Helen: I admired those women giving evidence. They were very nervous and worried about what they were supposed to do. But they stayed resolute. Their chins were up. Especially the one who looked like she was in a seance. I felt they conveyed Erin's desperation. What came out was a sense of her sadness around the marriage break-up and the sort of strictures of her life. Sarah, would that help the prosecution to explain why she'd done it?

Sarah: Through these witnesses, the prosecution is telling the jury that Erin had experience dehydrating mushrooms and hiding them in food. The prosecution doesn't have to prove motivation, but the stuff the women said about her animus towards Simon and his family would go towards intention.

And then, of course, the defence, when cross-examining the online friends, was trying, through repetition, to fortify a narrative of Erin as a good mum, a devoted parent. And, to a certain degree, to tarnish Simon's image as the blameless husband. That's tricky because they don't want to highlight too much her animus towards him. They just want the jury not to trust his version of the story. They're doing what they can with what they have.

Sitting on the side of the court, I could watch Erin in profile. She was expressionless, inscrutable. But then she looked like she might cry when one of her Facebook friends called her a good mother. 'All she really cared about in life was her children,' one said.

Today the conditions of Erin's cell were discussed in passing. There's a lot of logistics to holding a major trial in a regional court. Justice Beale mentioned he had checked the court facilities ahead of the trial. He described being taken to see the cell where Erin would be held and—this is what got me—finding that the bed was effectively a piece of plastic attached to the floor. There was a brief mention of her having her own sheet and pillow. I was left with this heaviness, for a fleeting second, of how everyone's going to leave the building each day, except her. And she'll be led away to sleep on a piece of plastic.

❖

According to the newspapers, Erin had described her upbringing to her Facebook friends:

> My mum was ultra weird her whole life. We had a horrible upbringing. Mum was essentially a cold robot. It was like being brought up in a Russian orphanage where they don't touch babies.
>
> Dad wanted to be warm and loving to us, but Mum wouldn't let him because it would spoil us, so he did as he was told. She would shout at him if he did the wrong thing, so he became very meek and compliant. My sister and I would hide in our room most of the time so we couldn't do the wrong things.

Chloe: Erin said that, to cope with this, she spent most of her childhood reading. It stuck in my head that her mother, Heather Scutter, was a professor of children's literature at Monash University. I went to the State Library on Saturday to see if I could find anything she'd written. There were a couple of years in the 1990s where Heather Scutter appeared in the *Women's Book Review*, a feminist periodical, almost every month. It's interesting hearing her voice.

Sarah: Do you believe what Erin says about her mum being a robot?

Chloe: I don't know. Erin's tone is often self-pitying. I believe it less when I read Heather's work.

The September '93 issue cover has the title *Is That You Mum? Revisioning Motherhood* and a Victorian illustration of a woman with children nestled beside her and a puddle of kittens in her lap. The editorial begins, 'In this issue we turn our attention to the myriad representations and implications of motherhood. The facts of motherhood and non-motherhood shape the lives of women in both direct and subtle ways.' And then it goes on to talk about the impact of capitalism, imperialism and technology on women's experiences.

So inside is Scutter's article, which is called 'Choose Your Own Madonna'. It's a review of various young adult novels and it opens with the line, 'There's reactionary nostalgia in the air as far as mothers go in children's fiction…too many snap-frozen mothers from an imagined past. The ideal home and garden has a present mum with an absent mind.'

In the next issue, which is called *In Praise of Bolder Women*, she writes, 'Writers have to be variously talented to bring in the bread and butter. How do writing women survive?'

Helen: They go on the road.

Chloe: Yeah, we need to chip in for the petrol, Sarah. So Scutter was very interested in constructions of gender. She's writing about domestication and submission and the ways in which women are typecast in post-colonial society. And she writes that she was previously a schoolteacher. She describes herself as a reading mum, and talks about the books that her children loved. And it's done through a feminist lens.

Helen: Her mother sounds like one of those kick-arse feminists of my generation.

Chloe: Erin's father was Jewish—so she's not without any religious tradition. But her problem was with her mother. If you were the child of a feminist, atheist academic, what is the greatest rebellion that you can have? Move to 'the sticks', marry a Baptist and stay home with your kids?

Helen: Hearing you read out those articles, I look back on that sort of feminism as…doctrinaire. There was a lot of theory. We were always applying rules to each other.

Chloe: Like a Baptist.

Helen: Erin's mother was extremely prolific. Pumping out those articles. She's tough.

Chloe: Indulge me on this, but mushrooms often appear in children's literature. Beatrix Potter was a mycologist.

They are used as little houses. They're characters in certain books. They're also used in potions. Food in these stories has a transformative effect; people cook or are fed magical or poisonous things that make them become other things—in Erin's case, she'd morph from being someone feeling beleaguered in Korumburra. So, it's strange to me that Erin couldn't bear her mother and rejected that childhood, and yet this has elements of a fairy story her mother might have read to her, with a forest and witchiness and food changing in front of the guests in a deadly way.

Through the car windows we can now see the outer suburbs of Melbourne, and it's growing darker.

Helen: I'm thinking about the tension between the couple. It was weird to go into the courtroom and see they were within metres of each other. I never saw Simon look in her direction. I saw her looking over at him and the family she'd once been part of.

Chloe: Do you think she's got *anybody* who believes she is innocent?

Sarah: I reckon she would. At least one of those Facebook women.

Helen: Maybe she's one of those really smart women who are a little bit crazy and whose emotional lives are hard for their friends to bear. You couldn't really imagine having a peaceful friendship with her. No wonder she socialised online.

Sarah: I wasn't surprised to learn all those friendships were with women she had never even met for a coffee. I'm thinking of distance again, how poisoning is damage you inflict at a remove.

Would it be feasible to argue that she intended to just make the lunch guests really sick? That was the other bit in the data about the female poisoners—sometimes it wasn't intended to be lethal. It was to control somebody from a distance by making them sick.

Helen: I reckon she would have researched the right dose. I reckon that she would've gotten a thrill from researching it and having that power.

Chloe: (*checking on her phone*) Consuming just one death cap mushroom can kill an adult.

Sarah: I keep thinking about psychological poison—the way the emotions that drive murder grow in darkness. Like mushrooms. All the dark feelings and personality traits we're taught to hide or be ashamed of lurk there, in our psychic shadow. It raises the idea of the two faces. Who was Erin to her friends? Who was she to the family, at church, as a wife, as a daughter? Where did it come from? *Where* do you start the story? Like, why is she even in that tiny courtroom and not controlling aeroplanes in the sky?

As for that bit they mentioned about Simon's parents placing demands on her—that's the flip side of belonging and inclusion. Perhaps that had started to chafe.

Helen: When the witness from the Facebook group spoke about him as being coercive and controlling, I thought of his face and saw it differently. It was the same face and it was the same composed expression that he had on the stand, but suddenly I thought, With a guy like that it might be really hard to change his mind about anything. Who knows how much of that toughness has come to him since what has happened? It's impertinent even to guess.

Chloe: The more straightforward Simon is, the more devious she is. The story is different depending on how much you shade each of them grey.

Sarah: The way he tells it, she's the one in control, always leaving him, and in her story he is the one trying to control her.

Chloe: This is why people have attached so strongly to this case. Everyone knows how acrimonious things can get between ex-partners.

Helen: When my marriage was breaking up, I was going to a therapist, who said to me, 'You've got the habit of bolting when things go wrong.' She said, 'What you need to learn is you have to live the thing out to the end.' And it hit me, you can't just walk out of a marriage. You have to blast your way out, or burrow your way out, or dig your way out.

Chloe: Well, Erin bought her own house.

Helen: Yeah, but I'd like to know what pressure she might have been under, even after they separated. Was there pressure to come back? Divorce, for a practising Christian…

I look at some people I've seen in the dock, and I think, Jesus, I've been there, and somehow I didn't crack—something in me stopped me from cracking and murdering. I remember when that poor Sudanese woman, Akon Guode, drove her kids into the lake. It was picked up on CCTV that she drove around and around and around the water in this big SUV full of small kids. And then she stopped, and she put her head on her arms on the steering wheel, and the kids were going crazy in the back. And I thought every mother in this world knows that moment where you think, God, I can't stand this any longer. A friend of mine said to me, 'I have to know why she broke.' That's what I'm always looking for in these stories. What was the point at which Erin just could not hack it any longer?

Chloe: She has elements of a fantasist or fabulist. Who knows what she's told herself about breaking.

Sarah: If she's found guilty, I'd be surprised if she participated in a psych evaluation for sentencing. I think she would refuse to do that. She could come to believe that she's innocent, either completely or in the sense of being justified. That's how that kind of fantasy life works.

Helen: I feel even more confused now than when we started out...

Oh, that's where you did that daring U-turn this morning.

Sarah: We've come back to where we started.

Helen: This time in darkness.

Sarah: I wouldn't want to go there with anyone else.

PART II

The Church and the House

Friday, 9 May 2025

THE CURRENT OF THE story has a stronger pull than we had expected. Within a few days we are back on the M1 driving past the graffitied concrete cladding of the freeway walls. We have been sitting by our computers in Melbourne, listening via the media audio-link to the live testimony in the courtroom.

On Tuesday we'd heard Tanya Patterson, Simon's sister-in-law.

Sarah: She was a great, no-nonsense woman. It was interesting because she spoke frankly about the animus between Simon and Erin, without any sense of malice. She was just very plain spoken: 'Nah. For a year before the lunch, they barely spoke. And it got worse.'

The secretary and the treasurer of the Korumburra Baptist Church had visited the Wilkinsons after the lunch to discuss some church business. Heather, they told the court, had raved to them about how clever Erin was to have made the complicated dish of beef Wellington.

Chloe: Heather was surprised and slightly excited about the lunch because she'd never received an invitation from Erin before. The daughters of Heather and Gail both rang their mothers afterwards to ask how this unexpected meal had gone. Everyone seemed to say no more than, 'It was fine.' In my house, if an ex had been involved we would be, to borrow your word, Sarah, *kvetching* for hours, psychoanalysing everything, even the napkins on the table.

Helen: Yeah, we would too. I imagine in this family you had to apologise for raising your voice, like Simon did in one of his text messages.

Sarah: I'm getting that theirs is not an externalising culture. It's very respectful. No one talks about what you'd imagine would be the first thing they'd talk about.

Chloe: Is it the legal or the religious framework—speak no evil—that means the family can't talk about their impressions of aggression? That it has to be only bland factual details? It's hard to grasp there was a person with potentially murderous intent and no one seems to have noticed.

Sarah: There was no indication in anyone's voice that hot

emotion was running through them. They had every reason to be hateful and angry.

Chloe: The law compresses emotion. These huge feelings are contained in that weird box.

Helen: The box itself makes demands on people. This is a struggle between the law and our wildness.

When I heard Ian Wilkinson describe Erin serving the meal that would kill his wife, I bawled. He sounds such a gentle person, and he had that little nervous laugh when he spoke.

The day had started like any other. Ian and Heather Wilkinson had been at their daughter's place the night before to celebrate their son-in-law's birthday. He had just bought a smoker and the family were eating smoked meats he'd prepared for his party, along with roast vegetables. On Saturday morning the Wilkinsons sat down to breakfast.

'I have porridge basically every morning for breakfast so I probably had a nice bowl of porridge,' Ian said. Heather more typically had toast. Then they took their usual Saturday morning walk together. 'We would buy the newspaper. On this particular day, we did that, and we continued on to the Burra cafe, where we had an appointment with our neighbours to have a coffee.'

Sarah: Helen and I texted 'a nice bowl of porridge' to each other at the same time, and I knew she had teared up too. It's those tiny, quotidian details that contain the world—we can all relate to them.

Helen: My heart broke for him. And that's why it's a good idea to have somebody in a collaborative group like old tough boss over here.

Chloe: Thanks.

Helen: No, truly, because I need to be hosed down. I need to have near me, in these kinds of stories, somebody who's slightly less overwhelmed than I am. The older I get, the more I agree with the Buddhists. Life is suffering.

I don't feel I've got a rational grip on this story. I just don't get it. I look at her and I think, *What* is in your head and how did it get there?

I think Erin is a person who is overwhelmed by her emotions. She married into a family who knew how to discipline their feelings. It's the old Calvinist thing about child-rearing—break the will that will otherwise destroy you—

Chloe: —or others.

It's a squally day with grey skies. The concrete walls have given way to green paddocks. We're crossing the Little Moe River in Gippsland.

Chloe: There's a strange marriage going on in this car. We all cope differently with the intensely emotional aspects of this trial. I'm being painted as the hard arse, but perhaps we are organising ourselves into certain strengths.

Helen: I blatantly sent you a text, saying, 'Are we being sentimental, Chloe?'

Chloe: Should we talk about this? It was terrible hearing Ian Wilkinson's testimony. We could hear the shake in his voice and his nervous laugh at the end of certain answers. This man has turned up in court twenty-two months after waking from a coma to find his wife, his sister-in-law and brother-in-law all dead, allegedly murdered. He talked about knowing Erin, who was metres away from him in the dock, only on a superficial level. When he and his wife were invited to lunch, he felt pleased by the idea that perhaps it would improve or deepen his relationship with Erin. Heather prepared a fruit platter, and his sister-in-law baked an orange cake.

Erin hadn't ever invited them around. They'd turned up once before and come up the drive but had not been asked inside. It was exciting, now, to see inside this newly built dream house. The sisters, Heather and Gail, were leading the conversation. And you could see them, these country women, trying to settle everybody down and ease this, perhaps fairly awkward, social encounter. They made small talk while looking out at the garden. The older women were both keen gardeners, and they chatted with Erin about moving a plant that wasn't thriving. And then Heather wanted to see inside Erin's deluxe pantry because she was hoping to get a new pantry herself—

Helen: —and she was really interested in pantries. I loved that touch.

Chloe: But Erin wasn't keen to show it to her.

Helen: I don't think Ian meant there was anything sinister about the pantry. But he was surprised to find that Erin didn't fall in with the request…Well, I think he now considers it sinister.

Sarah: He was remarkably sensitive. He said he sensed some discomfort from Erin about the pantry, and he thought, Oh maybe it's a mess and she's embarrassed, so I won't go along and look. So he chatted with Don about some books on Erin's bookshelf.

Chloe: Presumably, the dehydrator was in the pantry, and that's where the death caps had been prepared.

Helen: You saw it like the witch's cave?

Sarah: I'm just thinking it's more broadly related to a deep discomfort with being seen or some kind of self-loathing or sense that she's going to fall short and—

Chloe: —Come on, guys, she's freaking about to poison them! I'm not saying there was a photo board with red strings in there, but this is where she constructed the terrible meal.

Helen: When you've made a plan like this, I wonder if that part of your mind is closed off from the rest—an area of your consciousness is heavily bearing down on the fact that you're about to do this thing and it's almost a secret from yourself.

Chloe: A kind of disassociation?

Sarah: I agree. We saw it in her statement when she was doorstopped by the media. She couldn't believe, or she was acting like she couldn't believe, that her relations had died. Some offenders end up crediting their own lies. There was no malice. No plan. No wrong done. They are not the person who planned it and executed it. The fantasy life is huge.

Helen: After they finished eating lunch, Ian said, Erin announced she had ovarian cancer. The guests were devastated. She said it was life-threatening.

Sarah: She asked everyone if they thought she should tell the kids. Ian said, 'In that moment, I thought, *This* is the reason we've been invited to the lunch.' And he led them in prayer.

❖

Dr Chris Webster testified that he was on duty in Emergency at Leongatha Hospital when the Wilkinsons arrived, vomiting but still lucid, the following morning. They were admitted.

That afternoon, Webster received a text message from a doctor at Dandenong Hospital, where Don and Gail had been taken by ambulance. Their condition was rapidly deteriorating, and they were about to be transferred across the city to the Austin Hospital, in the suburb of Heidelberg. Later that evening, Webster received a call from the Austin. The Pattersons' liver-function tests were 'grossly abnormal', and it was suspected they were suffering from death cap mushroom poisoning.

On Monday, 31 July, the Wilkinsons too were deteriorating, and Webster was organising their urgent transfer to the Austin.

At 8.05 am, just as the couple's ambulance was about to leave, Erin Patterson showed up at Emergency. She said she was suffering from diarrhoea.

Dr Webster asked where she had got the mushrooms for the beef Wellington.

'Woolworths,' she answered.

He told her she had likely been exposed to a potentially lethal dose of death cap mushrooms. Erin and her children, who, she told him, had eaten the lunch leftovers, needed urgent medical treatment.

Erin said she didn't want to scare her children by taking them to hospital.

Her kids, said Webster, could be scared and alive, or dead.

At 8.10 am, five minutes after she had arrived, Erin discharged herself from Leongatha Hospital. She told the staff she had urgent tasks to attend to and would return. Dr Webster called Erin three times. She did not pick up. Out of concern for Erin and her children, he phoned the police.

His Triple Zero call was played in court.

Erin walked back into Emergency ninety minutes later at 9.48 am. She told a worried nurse she wasn't overly concerned for the kids. She had scraped the mushrooms off the food she'd given them.

The police now phoned Webster. They were at Erin's house to do a welfare check but could not get in. He told them Erin was with him, then he had another thought. Webster asked Erin if the police could retrieve any leftovers for analysis. He passed the phone to Erin and she gave an officer her gate code and a description of the food scraps' location. Senior Constable Adrian Martinez-Villalobos, of Mirboo North Police Station, put on two pairs of latex gloves and collected one and a half leftover beef Wellingtons from the bottom of Erin Patterson's rubbish bin.

❖

Chloe: Erin, a disciple of true crime, is now the auteur of her own true-crime nightmare. Her beef Wellingtons have inspired an entire industry of death cap related productions. There are various companies making documentaries, another making a dramatised TV series. There are a dozen podcasts underway. Journalists are providing minute-by-minute online coverage. Books are being written. There's a huge economic imperative in the courtroom, and I'm conscious of our symbiotic place in the ecosystem. But I want to know more about true crime's appeal to women. I read that something like seventy per cent of Amazon's true-crime book reviews are by women, whereas for war books it's like eighty-two per cent men. A female audience is driving the production of true crime in every medium. Why are women so fascinated by this?

Sarah: Why do you think?

Chloe: Escape. You don't have to think about war or climate change or the bills you need to pay. Procedural crime shows begin with some sickness in the citizen body. There's a communal fear: will this murderous energy be contained? And, at the end, a clever detective manages to cauterise the rot and we can all sleep safely. I suppose true crime gives that relief with the added frisson of it being factual.

But there's another theory: women are listening to or reading or watching true crime because they recognise themselves in these stories as, unfortunately, the victims—most often—and they're almost trying to game out: How do you *not* pick the sociopath on Tinder? Just as fairy stories are cautionary tales, you know, you shouldn't hitchhike along a dangerous road in the middle of the night or you shouldn't—

Helen: —go into a scary motel.

Chloe: Yeah, I'm not completely convinced by that sort of social-use argument, but apparently women who consume true crime often tend to empathise with the perpetrators in an effort to understand their motives. In this case, the accused person is a woman. People are fascinated by female violence and that is age-old.

Helen: In order to live a life, women have to throttle back in themselves huge amounts of aggression. So I'm never surprised when I hear about a woman killing someone. It doesn't surprise me at all.

Sarah: There's a social taboo around female aggression—and often even assertiveness. These stories are about power. For women, who often don't have much of it in their own lives, that's fascinating.

We're now driving next to rolling fields.

Sarah: What's that? Those things tied to the fence?

Chloe: Dead foxes.

Sarah: Why would they hang them up?

Chloe: Hunters showing off their kill. It's meant to be a warning to other foxes.

Helen: For millennia, there were also public hangings.

❖

Chloe: When you google Medea, 'Medea, public figure' comes up. And it turns out, she was known as an accomplished *pharmakeia*. That's a Greek word for an expert in dark medicinal magic or potions, aka someone who poisons people.

Sarah: It's like we have DNA for stories like this.

Chloe: Her story first appears in 700 BC, so if Erin Patterson poisoned her relatives, she's one of a long historical line.

Helen: That she was a member of an honourable company, though, that might be pushing it.

I just want to know what happened in their marriage. I'm pretty sure I'm not going to find out from what is said in the court. I'm very interested in marriages and how they start off well, and everyone's happy and excited, and then something goes wrong and it becomes irreparable, and people have to give it up.

Chloe: It's the great subject in your diaries. But what do you think of the fact that Erin allegedly tried to kill two seemingly very happily married couples?

Sarah: Their happiness was striking. You could tell from Ian's way of speaking about his wife, his account of how they spent their days together.

Chloe: His simple way of telling the story, the beauty of his love for his wife, who was still working, teaching English to refugees, their pleasure in being invited out to lunch, the sense of faith that informed their life and their commitment to their family and the area—it was extremely moving. I admit, though, that every time somebody mentions beef Wellington, I hear a little bell of absurdity ring. It's such a flamboyantly retro dish. My partner's family comes from the town right next to Korumburra. He went to Korumburra High School. His mother's last big birthday bash was in the local Uniting Church hall. So I feel I know this milieu a bit—people's regard for traditional *Women's Weekly* or Country Women's Association dishes. But a beef Wellington has a feel of 1950s or '60s colonial grandeur. When I admitted this bell-ring to Sarah, she put me right beautifully. The reason this story is so compelling is that it has everything in it that's human, including absurdity.

Sarah: There is laughter in the courtroom. It's a workplace. Where people spend large amounts of time together, day in, day out, it happens. I've seen it again and again.

Chloe: It's also self-protection, trying not to get too ruined by the sadness. There is ageism, though. If Erin had poisoned four children, the atmosphere would be very different.

Helen: In court, which is supposed to be a solemn place, slack is cut for people. There's got to be some relief from the part of life that's so dreadful and violent and sorrowing and bestial. If you're not allowed to laugh, you might as well go and throw yourself under a truck.

I'm suddenly thinking of a line by the French writer, Jean Cocteau: 'What would I do without laughter? It purges me of my disgust.'

WE PARK NEAR THE Morwell Centennial Garden, which boasts hundreds of colourful roses. Across the street is the courthouse with a line of news cameras on tripods and reporters waiting for the day's first live-cross. The usually quiet town is full of journalists. We pass through the court security and look into the media overflow room where a large screen is set up in front of rows of office chairs. We find seats inside the courtroom.

The jury is shown prerecorded interviews between a detective and Erin's nine-year-old daughter, and then her fourteen-year-old son.

In the dock, Erin watches her own screen. She is crying very quietly. She wipes her eyes with a tissue.

Erin's daughter sits in an interview chair. She says that during the lunch she went to McDonald's with her brother and his friend. Afterwards they went to a movie. Their dad picked them up and dropped them home. Later that day, her mother told her she felt sick. 'She said that she had diarrhoea and her tummy was sore.' Before bedtime, they played on an iPad together. The next morning Erin said she was still ill. They skipped church and had a game of Monopoly.

Time has stopped in the courtroom.

There's a picture window that shows the rooftops of Morwell, then, past them, the old pit mine, then the purple Strzeleckis, then the sky.

Erin looks undone, she's trying to stay steady.

Erin's son says that he arrived at the end of the lunch and talked to his grandfather about aeroplanes. After the guests left, he and his friend played games all afternoon. On Saturday night his mother was alone in her room doing a Lego project. She told him she was feeling sick and needed to use the toilet a lot.

On Sunday, Erin's son was booked to take a flying lesson. Erin drove the two children to the Mornington Peninsula airport, an hour away. At the last minute the lesson was cancelled, and they all drove home again.

That evening, according to Erin, she felt too ill to cook. Instead, she served the leftovers from the lunch, scraping the mushroom paste off the meat in the beef Wellingtons.

Erin's daughter says her mother 'wasn't very hungry so she did not eat that much'. Her brother finished her mother's portion. The boy says it was the tastiest meat he'd ever eaten. On Monday morning, he came downstairs and his mother was drinking her coffee. She seemed quieter than usual.

Had he ever known his mother to forage for mushrooms? the detective asks.

No, says the boy, but he does recall walking with her during a Covid lockdown in Korumburra Botanic Park, where they saw some fungi growing. He remembers her telling him these mushrooms grew on the roots of trees and the organisms worked together to support each other.

❖

Fridays are shorter sitting days to allow the judge and lawyers to attend to work that cannot be done during court hours.

After court adjourns, we decide to drive to Korumburra, an hour away. We want to get closer to the epicentre of the story. Korumburra is where Ian Wilkinson is pastor of the Baptist church. Here, Simon and Erin worshipped along with his parents. Don Patterson was a much-liked and respected teacher at Korumburra High, and Gail Patterson did a lot of volunteering, including reading the newspaper to the blind. We're heading into the vista framed by the courtroom window.

Chloe: Right now, we're turning out of Morwell, passing the giant, obsolete machinery from the Hazelwood coalmine. This is a blasted post-industrial landscape. But soon we'll be on the other side of the Strzeleckis in a pastoral painting of gum trees and rolling hills.

I can remember my partner's mother turning to me and asking, with a note of reproach, 'Do you know Gippsland well?' She was a lovely woman, but it was like being asked 'Can you speak French?' or 'Do you ski?' I was ignorant about this region at the centre of the world.

Sarah: Should we talk about the evidence from today? Erin and Simon's kids?

Something I found almost unbearably sad was the timescale. The distance of nearly two years between the day of the police interview with the kids and now. Erin cried as she watched her children on screen from the dock. She's been in custody all this time. I felt like I was hit on the head with what those kids are carrying. But also with her loss. The kids described a routine Sunday night, having their showers and eating dinner and playing a game. And that hasn't happened again for all this time—she hasn't had a normal day with her children and they haven't had a normal day with their mum.

Chloe: Often the worst day of your life doesn't feel far away. You could almost go back and change one tiny thing. When you hear the children speak, you want it to be true that their mother could be innocent.

Helen: I wondered how this was affecting Erin, but I didn't dare to look around. I don't get a clear view of her partly because I'm sitting on those rather low seats inside and I can't see past the tall people. When court rose and everybody was filing out, I glanced over at her. She was talking to her counsel and his junior. Her face has changed since the famous footage of her standing outside her house and putting her hands over her face and turning and running away. She's lost weight in prison. There's a sort of drama in her face now despite the fact that she's often expressionless. One of the lawyers said something that made her laugh—a flash of mirth and she turned into a person.

Sarah: From where Chloe and I were sitting, on the side, we had a clear view without being rubbernecks. She's fifty, but there's something about her face, how she holds herself, that makes her look much younger. Not naive, but she exudes a childlike quality. She cried a lot. She wasn't sobbing, but you could see her eyelids and her nose were getting redder. I saw it when her daughter was talking. And then, when her son was speaking, her chin was quivering. She also nodded along at times with what they were saying.

Helen: When we got here on our first day, I had a feeling we were unwelcome. People weren't giving eye contact. A bunch of local women was standing round the outer door of Courtroom Four. I was worried they were all members or friends of the families and they were giving us dirty looks because we were there from the city to perve. But they were just shy. One of them smiled at me and everything warmed up and became friendly. Her name is Tammy. She told me she cleans houses. And the woman with the black overalls, Kelly, I like her. She's a dairy farmer. She told me how cool it is that she doesn't have to get up before dawn anymore because all their cows are milked by robots—I don't think she was pulling my leg. We all started talking in that womanly way about trivial home things, you know, 'I didn't think I could get here today because my kids were *blah blah blah*,' and everybody's laughing and you're getting the full solidarity of women. I can take any amount of that.

Chloe: Were they true-crime buffs?

Helen: They didn't seem to be, unless they were keeping quiet about why they'd come. They weren't analysing motivation with severe psychology, anyway.

Sarah: I reckon they must be. They were trading notes, like, 'No, that happened at 5.55.'

Helen: I felt great companionship there. Do you think it's because it's a woman's trial? That's why we're all here, isn't it?

Sarah: Maybe. In a lot of trials a certain camaraderie develops.

Helen: Well, there's the retro factor, like what you were saying about the Country Women's Association. That is pure, beautiful retro. I always go to the CWA room at the Melbourne Show. They say, 'Would you like a cup of tea, dear?' And I say,

'Yes, please. And would you adopt me as well?'

Chloe: And yet, Erin hadn't invited Simon's aunt into the house until that lunch.

Helen: So perhaps we're talking class here as well.

Sarah: I reckon.

Helen: Maybe we're talking education levels.

Sarah: Or city versus country. In a way, Erin's always going to be city.

Helen: Oh, God, I keep forgetting that. Yeah.

Chloe: Are we really going to drive past Erin's house? I feel unsure about this.

Sarah: For me, it's a normal part of doing research.

Helen: We're not knocking on anyone's door, for God's sake.

Sarah: I have never done that. But I think there's enormous value in getting a feel for a place. I'd usually come and look at a house and a neighbourhood as part of trying to understand the people—what it says about their daily lives—while trying, to the limited extent I can, to walk around in their shoes.

I don't feel comfortable writing a story unless I have an understanding of the scale of the people's lives, the way the light hits, the houses and shops, the feel of the thing.

Helen: We just have to drive past looking straight ahead

with stony faces, but with our eyes kind of going to one side.

Chloe: This trial is being used for public entertainment. I feel squeamish about joining the pile-on.

Sarah: That doesn't just reflect on the journos, it's also the readers.

Chloe: There's the noise of constant typing in the courtroom. It sounds like little critters, like some sort of insect, eating, eating, eating the story up: *nomnomnomnomnom…*

Sarah: Yeah. It's how you go about it—not just what you look at but how you look at it.

Chloe: A guy from one tabloid got stuck in Erin's garden when he was doorknocking. She closed her automatic gates and accidentally shut him in. At the time he had on a leg brace, and it took a while for him to get out. Whenever she sees him in the courtroom, she apparently gives him a dirty look.

Sarah: We're not chasing anyone down for comment. And we don't pressure anyone who doesn't want to participate.

Chloe: I raise this stuff, not to drag what we're doing down into the shit. I guess I'm just trying to understand the difference, quite earnestly.

Sarah: Okay, let's take the kids. How would we write about the evidence we heard today and yesterday? Obviously, there are suppression orders that prevent them being identified or described in ways that identify them. But the ethical issues don't even begin to be touched by that.

Chloe: Perhaps it's something that we try to float over, because the kids feel, to me, close to being the worst betrayed.

Sarah: They've been handed this bag of stones that they'll carry for the rest of their lives. And they were given them at nine and fourteen.

❖

We drive through the Strzelecki State Forest, once famous for its lyrebirds and mammoth trees. It's late autumn and the leaves of the European trees in the small towns are flaming orange and red.

Chloe: Sarah, tell Helen the story you heard about Erin taking industrial action.

Sarah: When she was working at the air-traffic-control job?

Chloe: Yes.

Sarah: Okay, so in 2001, Erin completed a training program and worked as an air traffic controller for eighteen months. I heard she wasn't well liked. She left her shifts early, making the job more stressful for her colleagues. When she was confronted about this, Erin's response was that her treatment was sexist or misogynist in some way. Eventually she was sacked. Erin took them to court for unfair dismissal, and got the union lawyer to represent her. At the hearing, the lawyer was surprised when the employers provided CCTV footage of her leaving early. The lawyer said, You didn't tell me what I needed to know. We're both union—like 'comrades don't do this to each other'. And Erin replied, 'Oh, but I'm not a union member.'

❖

Korumburra, according to a local historian, began as 'a stinking, unsanitary and violent mining camp on the forest frontier of the British Empire' and has grown into a 'peaceful and law-abiding town that is the service centre for a prosperous farming community'. The town's coalmine closed in the late 1950s and for decades Korumburra prided itself on being home to the biggest butter factory under one roof in the southern hemisphere.

There's a grandeur to the Edwardian and Deco buildings along the main street.

Helen: These old Australian towns are sort of raw-boned. They've got enormously wide streets, as if carriages with eight horses are going to come galloping down them.

Chloe: It has all the requisite faded glory, with the vacant shops and pub and football field—you could be hearing Cold Chisel's 'Flame Trees' as you drive along.

In country towns there are always hidden undercurrents

of desire. My partner discovered years later that someone he knew had been running a brothel in the scout hall.

We pass the Ned Kelly bakery and the community centre and the supermarket and the town hall.

Chloe: In the hall, at our last family function, there was incredible food, desserts almost from a bygone era. I texted a family member asking for a list, and she wrote back, 'Pineapple flummery jelly, jellied bramble berries, golden syrup dumplings, trifle, golden staircase pie, tapioca pudding or frogs' eggs.' All the women painstakingly make these family recipes. And so, when we heard of the orange cake taken along to the lunch and the smoked meats that were eaten at a relative's house, I recognised food as a great delight amidst general stoicism. When I think about how taciturn my Gippsland family is, in terms of talking about the psychology of other family members, or speaking ill of anybody, the Patterson family makes sense.

Sarah: So, let's go first to the Korumburra Baptist church.

Helen: I was wondering about the pastor when he gave evidence about his wife. He laughed softly and I thought he probably believes she's in heaven in the arms of Jesus. It would be comforting to believe that.

Sarah: There it is. Up ahead, the yellow building on the hill.

Helen: A very steep hill.

We drive up and park outside.

Helen: (*reading from her phone*) The church was built in the 1880s. Baptist congregations had spread throughout Gippsland following the Welsh miners who'd immigrated to work the region's coalmines. All over the world the Baptists followed the poor.

The church is still beautifully maintained. It is as though we've arrived just after a working bee. The surrounding lawn is carefully mown, and the timber exterior looks freshly painted. The building's elevated position gives it an imposing presence.

Sarah: The view of the hills is gorgeous from up here. It feels like it would have been a very happy place for them.

Chloe: What are those flowers?

Helen: Hydrangeas, and I don't know what those purple ones are, they look like a native.

Chloe: Let's think about what was happening inside the church. This is where Ian Wilkinson is the pastor, and where Erin and Simon Patterson were members of the congregation. It's where Erin supposedly had a spiritual awakening. A fortnight before the lunch, Erin attended a service. Just another Sunday. Simon's family was there. Ian was in the pulpit. Erin took a pew. Was she praying? Was she thinking of the death caps she'd collected? Ian was talking about knowing Jesus; it seems Erin was deciding whether to play God herself.

After the service, Erin approached Simon. She told him she had serious news regarding her health that she needed to discuss. She then came upon Simon's mother and aunt Heather together in the church. 'Just the two I'm looking for,' she said and invited the sisters and their husbands to lunch in a fortnight's time.

Helen: I'm just going to look at the sign over here. It's a painting of Jesus, striding out of his tomb into bright daylight.

The sign reads:
    He has risen.
    He has risen.
    He has risen.

Helen: The grave cloths, how beautifully he's rolled them up, as he goes out. He's born again. The sign also says, 'If Easter says anything to us today…

Sarah: '…you can put Truth in a grave but it won't stay there.'

For the year before the lunch, Erin Patterson lived in her Leongatha dream house on a large block in a quiet, pleasant, semi-rural neighbourhood. As we roll along the unsealed road and approach the house, a subdued feeling falls over the car. We pull up outside the light grey, two-storey house with white trim, a sweeping veranda and modern windows.

Helen: It seems to be in a dark place. Am I projecting that?

Sarah: Well, look at the immediate neighbour. Their block has been cleared, it's a lovely expanse of green lawn and it has a completely different feel from Erin's. Her house is in its own little forest. It's a stark difference.

Behind a wire fence is the broad driveway and the carport where Erin Patterson was doorstopped by the media. Days after the lunch she stepped out of her car and into instant infamy by addressing a waiting pack in tears: 'It's a tragedy.

I'm so devastated by the loss,' she said, raising her eyes to the heavens. 'They are some of the best people I've ever met. They never did anything wrong to me…I just can't fathom what has happened. I just can't believe it.'

Her pleasant family home is now a crime scene.

Sarah gets out of the car to read a printed sign that is stuck to the gate.

Sarah: It says, 'Legal notice. Please be advised that the owner of this property hereby gives notice to all members of the media or any person employed or contracted to any media organisation that you are not permitted to enter any part of this property as marked by the boundary fence. If you do so enter it, then you are committing the offence of trespass— see section nine of the Summary Offences Act—and will be reported to the police.' Yeah, fair enough.

Helen: There are houses on this side, on quite large blocks, but on the other side there's a paddock.

Sarah: Her house is lovely. Kind of New Englandy, or beachy. No lawn. Is one of the paddocks hers?

Helen: It's a big block. Plenty of trees.

Chloe: But there's the actual reality of four people being poisoned in there, going inside cheerfully…

Sarah: What's that car doing behind us?

A large black SUV with tinted windows has pulled over on the verge, as if waiting for us to leave.

Sarah: What do you want to do? You want to hightail it?

Chloe: I think we should hightail.

Helen: Look at that banksia bush.

Sarah: We've got this car behind us. It's a bit creepy on a small dirt road. I mean, we are allowed to be here. We're not doing anything wrong.

Chloe: I feel weird being here…but who is in the car? Is it a vigilante neighbour?

Sarah: Are they flashing their lights at me? I'll get back onto the road. I want to know how short the drive was from here to the Woolies where she says she bought the mushrooms, to the Maccas and the cinema where the kids were during the lunch, and also the hospital.

Helen: Pretty convincing reason.

Chloe: Driving down the street, the whole time I felt, Don't do this. Don't go, please. I don't want to see the house! But then there was a creeping sense of curiosity: I wonder what it looks like. That's the creepy thrill you get from true crime.

Sarah: Well, would you feel comfortable reading something about a real place the author had never been to, never seen for themselves? Like, would you trust their accuracy?

Helen: No, I see your point. I was scared someone was going to get out of the car and say, 'Get out of here. We know why you're here. Fuck off! Who do you think you are?'

Sarah: I'm sure they're sick of people coming to have a look.

Helen: What if someone came out and said, 'Please don't hang around. Look, people come here all the time. Hanging around makes us really unhappy. Would you please go away?' If they said that, I would immediately go away, and I would feel sorry that I had come.

Sarah: Even if we are perving, I think there's a difference between knocking on someone's door and driving the roads, taking in the surroundings.

Helen: It was uncanny that a massive black SUV...

Chloe: ...with dark windows, came along and ushered us out.

Helen: They may have also been trying to perv at the house. They might not have been neighbours at all. The house looked uninhabited to me, don't you think?

The house, we later discover, is inhabited. Erin's power of attorney, another woman from her true-crime Facebook group, has moved in. Although the two had not met before Erin was charged with triple murder, the Facebook friend comes to court to support Erin most days.

Helen: Let's go home now. We're all tired, and it's a long drive.

Can we try to get straight the prosecution's case as we know it? The idea that she got rid of the famous dehydrator is very bad. Don't you think it looks really, really suspicious?

Four days after the lunch, Erin drove thirteen minutes from her house to the Koonwarra Transfer Station. CCTV footage shows her pull up in her red car and remove the dehydrator from the boot. She deposits it in an otherwise empty electronic waste bin. After it was retrieved by police, as Nanette Rogers had said in her opening address, forensic testing revealed both Erin's fingerprints and traces of death cap mushrooms. The prosecution also claimed Erin had downloaded information about where death caps were growing. Phone records suggested she had then travelled to these places.

Chloe: Her counsel's argument is that this poisoning was a mistake. And, in her panic, she got rid of the dehydrator. But we don't know what else he's going to bring out.

Sarah: He'll probably say that she was a clever but amateur forager—which is not a crime. And that, sadly, this tragedy happened. She lost her beloved in-laws and even made herself sick, and that there's no proof that she intended to do it. Colin Mandy is working with what he has and that doesn't seem to be a lot, but it's difficult to prove intention beyond reasonable doubt. Panic—that she freaked afterwards because it would look like she intended to kill them—can be an effective get-out-of-jail-free card.

Helen: Is it all circumstantial?

Chloe: Yes, but there's a *lot* of it. So, Sarah, you're Erin's lawyer. Might you have said to her, 'Listen. I'm going to be frank. This looks really bad for you. If you were to plead guilty now, you might be able to see your children sooner'?

Sarah: Maybe. The earlier you plead guilty, the bigger your potential for sentence discount—which could be between twenty and thirty per cent. You won't be penalised for pleading not guilty, but that discount recognises the benefit of having spared victims and witnesses the trauma of a trial. Still, at the end of the day, her counsel has to follow her instructions. I mean, if they know she's guilty they can't make arguments inconsistent with that, because they have a duty to the court, but she's entitled to put the Crown to proof. Trials are the exception nowadays. They're so extraordinarily costly. Most charges end up resolving in a guilty plea. But the personality that commits a crime like this is the same personality that believes they can get away with it.

Helen: Look at the cattle up on that hill. They're all spread out in a lovely way. What are those black ones called?

Chloe: Angus?

Helen: We don't even really care—about cows. Let's stop pretending. Have either of you been looking at the jury?

Sarah: Yesterday, I didn't see any of them looking over at her at all. They might feel intimidated or even scared to look. But today, especially when the son's video evidence was being played, they did look at her. We don't know what they're thinking.

Chloe: One of the journalists told me she was surprised when I said I didn't think Erin could be innocent. Her theory—pretty bizarre—is that possibly Simon snuck death cap mushrooms into her kitchen.

Helen: What? You're joking.

Chloe: She was thinking like a scriptwriter.

Helen: I'm amazed at how much makeup and hair action goes on in the overflow room.

Chloe: It's a strange thing that we get attractive young reporters to detail the most gruesome crimes—it's like Red Riding Hood with the wolf's carnage behind her.

Sarah: I watch them full of relief that, on top of everything, I don't have to worry about looking and sounding perfect as they do. They can't fuck up any details or violate any of the orders, and they're doing it all on camera in real time. What they have to hold in their head is huge.

Chloe: Whereas the male crime-journalists look grizzled and broken.

Helen: Everybody should smile less, especially women, in public. Every advertisement or commercial is full of people smiling with unnatural vehemence, and it drives me insane.

Chloe: Women often smile, ironically, to appear defanged.

Sarah: This goes back to our uncomfortable relationship with female aggression. Maybe true crime is a place where you don't have to do the smiling and mincing with the voice rising up at the end.

Chloe: Do we take women seriously? Was Erin taken seriously?

Helen: I suspect she wasn't taken seriously. I think she was seen in that family as a wild card. I mean, look at the two women who died of the poisoning. They were nanna-figures with little, neat haircuts and natural expressions of pleasantness.

Sarah: The other thing about those women is that they seemed content. But it's not just that Erin was a wild card, she's also undeniably intelligent. I'm not undercutting the decision to be a stay-at-home mother—it's just she had a lot of unused intellectual energy. Perhaps she was not being respected or recognised in the way she felt entitled to be, or in the way her own mother was. So where does that energy go—into frustration or resentment or a weird sense of superiority or researching the hell out of mushrooms?

Chloe: In her Facebook messages, she radiated discontent. She portrayed a desperate family situation. But here is somebody obsessed with crime stories, who is perhaps unhinged. A criticism of true crime is that it desensitises us to murder. Erin knows the tropes of the crime genre, and it sounds like she went and got herself burner phones, et cetera, to commit 'the perfect crime'. Actually, she almost managed it. Simon nearly died and no one was able to determine the cause. She posted pictures of mushrooms in her dehydrator. Do you think there was something performative about what she was doing? Was she putting on a show for these true-crime buffs?

Sarah: We don't have their replies, but from the tone of Erin's messages to her Facebook group, you can tell that she feels heard by women who understand, in broad terms, the nature of her frustration. In return, she's getting responses like, 'You're not crazy', 'We hear you', 'That's terrible'. I'm not saying they were urging her on, but instead of making her feel calmer they probably fed her anger. None of them could have guessed what the consequences would be—or even who they were dealing with.

Helen: In those groups, you're completely free to create a persona. It's a gathering of personas, rather than of real people.

Helen: This is a very energy-consuming thing that we're doing. It's not often that you talk and argue all day with people you like and you can flash with and get somewhere.

Chloe: I don't know if you can critique true crime while you're making it, but there's a funny thing when we disagree—it's like an external version of the arguments you have with yourself while writing as you try to decide what to put on the page.

Sarah: So there's an alternative to those impossible conversations that go round and round and round and round, holding everything in your head alone?

Turns out, I can collaborate with other people, but only if they're these two people.

Chloe: This collaboration is a trial, as in, an experiment. I hope we're not going to get out of the car at the end and also think it was a trial of our relationship. But what if the 'I' voice becomes 'we' on the page? Can it give the work a bigger scope?

Sarah: Do people ask you if it's lonely to work by yourself? I've never felt that.

Helen: I love working by myself. If anyone comes to my office, I'm furious. When I'm there, I shut the door. I need that solitude. I need that much more than I need to collaborate with people. I don't know if this is going to work, but I'm loving trying it, and I find it enriching and…Oh, there's a crash just up in front of us.

PART III

The Death Cap
(Amanita phalloides)

Tuesday, 13 May 2025

Helen looks up reviews of a motel in Morwell and finds this claim:

Disgusting...

Room dirty, blood all over the walls...

Walked in and walked back out straightaway...

She books instead into the Nightcap, a 1970s-era brown-brick motel at the back of the Morwell pub. Sarah needs to stay home to work on another project. Helen and Chloe check in and have dinner in the pub.

Kino numbers are on a screen above the bar. There's a children's area with a jungle gym full of plastic balls. Country music plays, but the pub is largely empty save for those taking advantage of pensioner-discount meals.

Chloe and Helen return to their room and call Sarah.

Chloe: The guy at reception said, 'You realise there's only one bed in the room.'

Helen: And Chloe said, 'You're not going to put the moves on me, are you, Helen?' Of course not!

Chloe: He also said, 'I've had that many prank calls asking if we serve beef Wellington. I say, "Come on, mate—can't you think of anything original?"'

All right, Sarah, we now have two beds and we're going to get our notebooks out and tell you about the day.

Sarah: Was it as crowded? Were the same women there again today?

Helen: The one whose cows are milked by robots was there.

Chloe: There were more onlookers, and the informant, Detective Eppingstall, saved the first few rows for the family members.

Helen: The first witness was a friend of Erin's son.

Chloe: His statement was read by the prosecution.

Helen: This boy had been at the movies with the Patterson children during the lunch. The kids all came home together just as the guests were about to leave. The friend heard Don Patterson and his grandson discuss planes and flying. 'Erin just seemed like her normal self to me,' he said. The boys spent the rest of the day playing video games.

Chloe: The next witness statement was also read. This was Ulysses Villalobos. He was the instructor giving Erin's son flying lessons.

Helen: I still can't believe the kid was flying a fucking plane!

Chloe: The day after the lunch, when Erin had driven almost an hour to the Mornington Peninsula airport, Villalobos called at the last moment to cancel.

Sarah: Not sure that you would drive two hours return if you had severe diarrhoea.

On Monday, 25 July, Erin was taken 112 kilometres by ambulance from Leongatha Hospital to Monash Medical Centre. Health workers were now carefully monitoring her symptoms and it was noted she did not have diarrhoea during the ninety-minute trip. Doctors at Monash found her to be clinically well with no signs of poisoning.

Erin was given IV fluids and a drug to protect her liver.

Chloe: Professor Rhonda Stuart gave evidence. She was trying to make sure there was no public health issue, and asked Erin if she'd been foraging. Erin denied it and told her she'd bought the mushrooms from Woolworths and an Asian grocery in Oakleigh or Glen Waverley. Later she told others it was Clayton or Mount Waverley. Then there was a toxicology registrar…

Helen: …a very chic doctor called Laura Muldoon. She said Erin reported nausea and diarrhoea, although her bloods and vital signs were all normal. She also asked Erin if she'd been foraging. Erin told her the mushrooms came from a Chinese grocer.

When questioned further by hospital staff, she told them she had used a combination of sliced button mushrooms and dried mushrooms to make the mushroom paste for the beef Wellington and she stated again that she had bought the dried mushrooms from an 'Asian grocer'. A child protection worker visited Erin in hospital and judged that the children could remain in her care.

The beef Wellington leftovers had arrived in two zip-locked bags at Monash Medical Centre with Erin. Dr Muldoon sent them to the National Herbarium at the Royal Botanic Gardens.

Sarah: They travelled by urgent taxi, unaccompanied leftovers full of poison.

A tall, slim man with a long grey beard and long grey plait wandered into the court and took the witness stand. Dr Tom May, the head mycologist and curator of the fungal collection at the National Herbarium, had to be called back from a brief walk. He was asked by the prosecution to tell the jury about death cap mushrooms, otherwise known as *Amanita phalloides*.

The death cap, he said, is predominantly pale green to pale

yellow, tending towards an olive or bronze colour. It has small white patches on its well-developed cap and white gills underneath. It has a high stalk with a free edge. It grows paler after rain.

Detectives from the Homicide Squad had originally visited Dr May, asking for help identifying photographs of mushrooms they had found on Erin's devices.

May told the jury he'd posted or annotated posts of more than thirty thousand mushrooms on iNaturalist, a website where citizen scientists post images of interesting natural phenomena. In a twist of fate, he mentioned that some months before the infamous lunch he had been in Gippsland himself at a conference in the small farming community of Outtrim, ten minutes from Korumburra. During his stay he had gone walking. He'd seen some death cap mushrooms and had uploaded photographs of them to iNaturalist, using the moniker Funky Tom. Those images were accessed on Erin's device.

Chloe: When the mycologist started, Erin had her glasses on. She seemed engaged in some new way during this evidence. Did you notice that, Helen?

Helen: I didn't. I had to crane my neck to look at her.

Chloe: We know Erin was an obsessive researcher. Who better to rely on for the location of *Amanita phalloides* than a world-famous mycologist? She wouldn't drive to just anyone's sightings of death caps, but she'd have trusted that May knew his stuff.

In her opening address for the Crown, Nanette Rogers had told the jury that when police searched Erin's house, seizing numerous electronic devices, they discovered she had downloaded two locations of death caps in Gippsland.

Retired pharmacist Christine McKenzie spotted death cap mushrooms while walking with her grandson on the Loch football ground, fourteen kilometres north-west of Korumburra. McKenzie had worked for twenty years at the Victorian Poisons Hotline and, knowing a bush kindergarten operated nearby, she collected as many death caps as she could in a doggy poo bag to dispose of them later. She posted her sighting as a warning on iNaturalist on 18 April 2023. Erin had downloaded these images and, in court, Tom May verified that the mushrooms were almost certainly death caps.

Helen and Chloe are still on the phone with Sarah.

Chloe: I was struck by the mycologist's imagery. The death cap was accidentally introduced into the Australian environment and exists in an 'obligate relationship' with oak trees: it is bound to the tree in order to survive. Erin too was introduced into the community and needed this oak-like family in ways she didn't fully understand.

Sarah: Tom May said death caps are hard to distinguish from non-lethal mushrooms. It takes a lot of experience. It made me think of discernment more broadly. There's no bright line with mushrooms, like there's no bright line with people.

Chloe: The fungal spores are always there in the soil, and then the mushroom suddenly shoots out. Just as there's always murderous intent, and sometimes you can see it with the naked eye.

Helen: Everything becomes a metaphor in a story like this.

Chloe: May went through the documented deaths by *Amanita phalloides* in Australia. About twenty have been recorded in the last thirty years. And somebody's cocker spaniel was found dead with a death cap in its mouth.

Helen: The defence is really stressing how hard it is to identify mushrooms.

Chloe: Yeah, as in she must have misidentified a few, and put them in the jar with the 'Asian' mushrooms that she had bought. The mycologist said that when you first pick death caps they smell almost sweet, but after they're dried the odour is very unpleasant.

Helen: They would have stunk the house out.

Sarah: There's a whole range of actions that indicate guilt, but that's not the only thing foraging can indicate.

Chloe: 'Erin, why were you accessing photographs of death cap mushrooms?'

Sarah: 'I wanted to know what *not* to pick. I thought—

Chloe: '—it was a stubble rosegill mushroom.

Helen: 'Or a shaggy parasol or a gigaspora.'

There was so much evidence, though, and often it just didn't seem to be going anywhere. How about the juror tapping his fingers on the jury box?

Chloe: Tapping out, *yeah, get on with it.*

Helen: *Come on. Come on.*

Chloe: I noticed Erin look over at that.

Helen: I keep thinking that her counsel must have, in some underground bunker, an enormous weapon, like Hitler's enormous weapon at the end of the war, when he said, Don't worry, it looks like we're getting thrashed but we've got this weapon, and when we put it into action, then we'll see the fur and feathers fly! I think, Where's this going?

Chloe: Dr Rogers showed a heat map of where in the world death caps exist.

Helen: And the country that, in fact, has none is China.

Chloe: So Erin's claim that she bought the mushrooms in a Chinese grocery takes another blow.

Helen: Rogers shot holes in that.

Sarah: That the defence is sticking with the Chinese grocer story—which I believe is racist—really beggars belief.

Helen: The mycologist is smart, but he's a bit of a mumbler. It was as if he exuded a soporific gas. I wasn't the only person going to sleep. It's very hard to feel that anybody's got a *grip* on this case. Is that your feeling too?

Chloe: I think Nanette Rogers has a pretty firm grip, but time warps in a courtroom. People were openly yawning as we heard about mushrooms' different gills and frills. Even Erin was fighting at one point to keep her eyes open.

Helen: This whole thing seems so laboured and heavy-footed.

Sarah: I'm sympathetic to Rogers because of the high volume of information she has to lay out, all interconnected and laden with significance. She's extremely detail-oriented, which I respect greatly. But sometimes—with the jury and the public—that can have diminishing returns. In a trial, you get the opening, and that's a story, and you get to closing, weeks later, and that's a story. But in between you get only bits of evidence admitted through various witnesses and documents, and they don't always signal where they're going. She doesn't get to connect everything up until the end. It's a jigsaw puzzle with no picture to follow.

Helen: I had an unnerving feeling sitting in the court today, like standing in water when the tide's turning. Turning slowly but with strength and flowing the other way.

Sarah: Away from guilt or towards guilt?

Helen: I feel that Mandy is getting a grip. And I didn't expect this to happen. I thought that Rogers was going to wipe the floor with him. Today I just couldn't seem to pin down what was happening. I didn't know if anything was even happening. And then I started to get that creepy sense of the beginning of a rip around your legs. And I thought, God, is this his special super weapon? The idea that Erin really was keen on foraging. That finally something was engaging her attention in a full way. And picking the death caps really was an accident.

Wednesday, 14 May 2025

CHLOE PULLS OPEN THE motel-room curtains to reveal a large, obsolete satellite dish and, beyond that, fog.

Helen: I woke up early and I was thinking a lot about the trial, and then I thought, Chloe's so soundly asleep, but what if she's not asleep? What if she's dead? How could I get out of having been the one who did the murder? If I'm the only other person in the room?

Chloe: I love that you thought, What if she's dead? Then, How am I gonna get away with it?

The fog sort of describes the trial. There's just a feeling of desperation in the end, isn't there. Everyone's incomprehension of the mycology evidence, and you can feel the family's deeper incomprehension of *why*.

Helen: That's the big stopper for me. It's so meticulous—making the powder. Going and getting a dehydrator.

Chloe: I bet everyone's thinking, How did she think

she'd get away with it?

Helen: Maybe she went into some kind of other mental state. I read that the poets Sylvia Plath and Anne Sexton used to talk endlessly together about methods of suicide. And they both did it. Could you get like that about murder? Like nothing else was real?

Chloe: It is almost a type of suicide, going through with murder, committing yourself to being removed from your children for a life in prison.

Helen: What would you call that? A state like that? It must have taken quite some time, weeks and months.

Chloe: It's funny that she decided to make up a story about cancer for the guests, because it's like a cancer, having such a murderous fixation.

Helen: *Fixation* is the word I'm going for, because I don't see why she would do it to the pastor and his wife. Maybe, if she had any reason for all this, any feelings against anyone, surely it wouldn't have been against them?

Chloe: There's a matricidal quality to killing off your mother-in-law and her sister.

Helen: It's as close as Erin could get to her real mother. She was already dead.

Chloe: Well, she had also planned to have Simon at the lunch. It was as though she wanted to get rid of all the people who perhaps she felt had taken her old life away.

Helen: I imagine there might be considerable severity with Baptists. But remember Simon saying that Erin ran out of the church in tears. Whenever I read about someone struck by a spiritual thunderbolt, I feel extremely interested and sympathetic. I was at church once with Tim Winton, and we sang that fabulous Wesley hymn that goes, 'Long my imprisoned spirit lay/Fast bound in sin and nature's night/Thine eye diffused a quickening ray/I woke, the dungeon flamed with light'. The next line is 'MYYYYY CHAINS FELL OFF', and everyone shouted it joyfully. People were laughing.

Chloe: There's a sort of S&M connotation, but yeah, please. I'd love my chains to fall off.

Helen: Take this load off me. I think people accumulate a lot of grief and guilt. Everyone's hauling a tonne of it.

Chloe: And you mean shame by that, as well?

Helen: Shame, yeah. But maybe guilt, rather than shame. By guilt, I mean the secret gnawing of all the horrible things you've done, whether anybody's noticed them or not, which is where shame is different. But I'm actually rather sympathetic to interpretations of Christianity that are not domineering or distorting, but do seem to have something to do with what Jesus said: 'I am come that they might have life, and that they might have it more abundantly.' That's the kind of line that I would like to follow. But I love the image of washing sin away. And all those Southern Baptist songs in the United States about going to the river. I'm sort of at ease with that. The whole Baptist aspect of this story is of great interest to me. But I'm not sure how interesting it will be to many true-crime-ish people who are watching this play out.

Chloe: But these are all important dimensions of the murders, aren't they? The nuance of what was important to the people who died.

Helen: Yes, for example, Ian Wilkinson, the pastor, the only one who survived, I'd like to know where he thinks his wife is now. Does he have that sort of religious belief—that sometimes can seem rather literal-minded, but which must be comforting in this kind of situation—that she's 'safe in the arms of Jesus'? Does he still believe in heaven? And, if so, does it relieve his grief? Is he angry? Does he feel it's his duty to forgive? What are his feelings as a highly developed Christian and as a pastor? What's in his heart? These aren't questions I can just barge up and ask.

When you spend a lot of time thinking about a case like this one, it's a world that you enter. It's separate from your ordinary life. And I'm feeling this particularly because we're in the Latrobe Valley and because it's far from home. It took me hours to get here when I came on the train. And when I step onto the territory of the court, which is going to make all these important decisions, I am awestruck.

Chloe: I think you feel the way other people might feel about church.

Helen: I have this awed feeling when I go into places where people are suffering openly. It's important to me to figure out a mode of being so that I'm not offending people, but neither am I turning away from them.

Chloe: A prayer for dignity.

❖

We have discovered the three of us are variously connected to Erin Patterson and the wider family. Helen knows a number of women who taught with Erin's mother, Professor Heather Scutter, at Monash University. Sarah knows one of Heather's students. Chloe's partner's niece and nephew were taught at Korumburra High by Don Patterson.

By chance, Chloe has also run into one of Erin's former classmates. Erin was educated in the accelerated stream for gifted students at University High School in Parkville, in the heart of progressive academic Melbourne. The classmate mentioned in passing that their friendship faded in their early teens when Erin became 'boy crazy…I liked boys, but not like *that*'.

Chloe: When you heard about this, Helen, you used the expression *Erin, c'est moi*.

Helen: I guess I had a pang of empathy, thinking, Oh, my God, she's one of those people, like me, who just are off the chain when they're young. Somebody who spent their youth rushing about doing crazy stuff, whatever it was, with some kind of reckless sexuality there. Maybe you meet a guy from a family who loves him and whom he loves, and who are kind people. You could see a marriage into a family like that as a refuge from your own craziness.

Do you think Erin knows that she's carrying the load of people's projections? Is that in itself a kind of awful sea that she's thrashing around in?

Chloe: She might feel the attention is her due.

Helen: There's a sort of charisma that hangs around people in such situations. Charisma is probably not quite the right word.

Chloe: It's a warped charisma. She's the most known woman in Australia right now.

Helen: Lindy Chamberlain was once the most known woman in Australia. And you look at those old press photos of her now, and you see enormous power radiating from her face—and, of course, she had not committed any crime and she knew she hadn't. That's another religious story—the

Chamberlains were Seventh-day Adventists—but what was projected onto her was outrageous.

Chloe: Erin will now feature in the lore of the land as a monster.

Helen: Absolutely. But what do we do if she's found not guilty?

Chloe: We'll have to rethink this whole project.

Helen: An old journalist once rang me up and told me about a story he was thinking of covering. He said, 'I can do politics, I can do economics, but I can't do crazy women. I think you should look at this story.'

Chloe: *Crazy women*—what an amazing line.

Helen: I made it less offensive. I think I called them women at the end of their tether.

Chloe: They're stories of people breaking.

Helen: Yeah, breaking that last little strand that holds them back from the abyss.

❖

Chloe: Erin had a striking moment with her counsel yesterday.

Helen: I saw her talking to him, and she was nodding her head for emphasis.

Chloe: He seemed to gesture over at you, as in 'Garner's in the court', and then Erin looked in your direction…I keep having this feeling that we're characters in Erin's story. She was enmeshed in all of these crime tales. And now she's got her own one, and we're sucked into it, and—

Helen: —and we're boosting it, we're giving it oxygen. We're breathing into it and shaping it, oh God.

Chloe: Well, it's interesting. The mycology book I'm reading, *Entangled Life* by Merlin Sheldrake, is all about not knowing who or what's actually in charge. Fungi, he says, 'confuse our concept of identity and force us to question where one organism stops and another begins'. He describes attending a South American conference where all the researchers became 'increasingly bewildered by the implications of our studies. Someone got up to talk about a group of plants that produced a certain group of chemicals in their leaves…However, it transpired that the chemicals were actually made by fungi that lived in the leaves of the plant. Our idea of the plant had to be redrawn. Another researcher interjected, suggesting that it may not be the fungi living inside the leaf that produced these chemicals, but the bacteria living inside the fungus. Things continued along these lines. After two days, the notion of the individual had deepened and expanded beyond recognition. To talk about individuals made no sense anymore.' Sheldrake sees all that is unknown about fungi as equivalent to a physicist's concept of dark matter making up ninety-five per cent of the universe. 'Dark matter and energy are dark because we don't know anything about them. This,' Sheldrake writes, 'was biological dark matter, or dark life.'

I know, I go off on these crazy tangents. You get to the guts faster.

Helen: I don't know what the guts of this story are, but the scientific things don't sort of fit the shape of my brain.

Chloe: I'm interested in the way fungi make up one interconnected system. Do you think religion is another one?

Helen: People can't endure the absence of some kind of map or plan. It's because everything is so enormous and complex and seething. This is why I never feel scornful about religion. I can see that it's an enormous poem of thinking, Why the fuck are we here? How did we get here? And what is my duty towards the other people that are here? Our commitments—like in marriage, for example.

I don't have any trouble visualising the Pattersons' marriage. I mean, I think she was probably sexy and funny and clever...

Chloe: ...and kind of wild and emotional.

Helen: Yes, and he was this Baptist boy...

Chloe: ...and she would have been exciting.

Helen: She must have shot into his consciousness, and shaken him up, shaken him out of his possibly prim obedience.

Chloe: But maybe she wanted that straitjacket for a while…

Helen: …and then his parents see their son get swept away by this hot little number—and I imagine to them she would be a lost soul and they'd want to save her. She was probably drawn to a family which, unlike her own family, functioned.

Chloe: I don't know if we can be sure that it's her family who didn't function, or whether she's the sort of person who brings dysfunction with her.

Helen and Chloe leave the Nightcap and drive down Morwell's main street to the courthouse. For decades the town revolved around the coalmine and power station. Now, eight years since both were shuttered, there's a quietness here that can feel eerie.

Helen: When we went to look at the church and we saw that rather touching Easter illustration of Jesus getting up and walking out of the tomb, do you remember how the shroud was neatly folded on the end of the stone bed? I made a note of it. It seemed significant to me. Somewhere in this story, there's got to be neatly folded grave cloths.

Chloe: Well, that's how carefully she went about her scheme.

Helen: When people fantasise about killing, they tend to stop at the death-dealing stroke. They're fixated on that. Their imagination doesn't go any further.

Chloe: Perhaps it's too total, the unreality of it. Could you have killed one of your ex-husbands when you were really, really angry?

Helen: No, but once I exploded with rage and wrecked a kitchen, and it was wonderfully gratifying. I threw a pot of beetroot soup against the wall. It looked like a giant bloodstain. I could have kept going! You can commit real destruction if you're only wrecking somebody's stuff.

Chloe: There are amazing stories, aren't there, of women, say, breaking into a man's house and cutting all his ties in half?

Helen: I guess they're all symbolic…

Chloe: …castrations.

Helen: Oh, the fog lying like a blanket over this sad town.

Monday, 19 May 2025

In the courtroom, we hear about horse mushrooms, honey mushrooms, shiitake and porcini. Exotic mushrooms, wild mushrooms, forest mushrooms, field mushrooms and 'just your basic button'. Slippery Jacks, young puffballs and the butter cap, or buttery collybia, which has greasy yellow pores and blue flesh. We hear about the hundreds of species within the *Amanita* genus, not just *Amanita phalloides*, but its 'close relatives' including *Amanitas eucalypti*, *gardneri* and *marmorata*—the marbled death cap. We hear about other mushrooms that also contain amatoxins—the genera *Amanita*, *Lepiota*, *Galerina* and also *Pholotina*. We hear about yellow stainer *Agaricus xanthodermus* and fly agaric *Amanita muscaria*, with its bright red cap and white warts, the gold top *Psilocybe subaeruginosa*, the shaggy parasol *Chlorophyllum brunneum* and ghost fungus *Omphalotus nidiformis*. We hear about how easy it is to mistake a death cap for the non-toxic *Volvopluteus gloiocephalus*, commonly known as the big sheath mushroom, rose-gilled grisette or stubble rosegill.

During the lunch break Helen and Chloe call Sarah.

Chloe: We're on a bench outside the bakery, Out of Dough. Helen's having a plain meat pie.

Sarah: When in Rome.

Chloe: In court, Erin has her glasses on and she's paying close attention to evidence, which other people find very dry. I feel it's more than just interest in her own case. She seems transfixed by the science of it. The defence barrister keeps putting photographs on the screen of mushrooms that look similar to death caps, ones Erin could claim she'd been foraging for. They were like mushroom pin-up or profile shots, every view and angle of their membranes and stalks and bulbous bits. The mushrooms lolling around the grass or standing straight on dried leaves. One woman literally pulled out her fan. I felt like I was hallucinating.

Helen: Well, you could say Dr May was pedantic. He would often make pronouncements like 'I'm aware that it needs some further taxonomic investigation'. And there was one moment when the barrister was saying, 'Now, this mushroom'—and there was a photo of it—'this mushroom's got a brown top.' And May says, 'Oh. I'm not sure if I would call that brown. It seems to me closer to a grey.' In the overflow room, a burst of shattering laughter.

Chloe: It was extraordinary hearing the turn this story has

taken into deep science. I was looking out the court window, thinking, We are surrounded by fungi. We're breathing it in. It's on our bodies. It's outside stretching under the ground. It has invaded the courtroom.

Helen: I had the exact same thought. I read about twenty pages of that mushroom book and every time I looked outside, was thinking, My God, there's always some fungi there, all joined up and growing. I feel quite wonderstruck and a tiny bit scared.

Chloe: We take it for granted, and yet it's far more important than we are…

Helen: …and we're just sort of wandering around on top of it.

Sarah: How close are death caps to where we all lie sleeping.

Chloe: It's entangled life, as Sheldrake puts it. Even this trial is connecting people. People are *obsessed*. I run into someone at my kids' sport, or the hairdresser, or wherever—they're either listening to two podcasts a day and know more detail about the trial than I do, or they're equally as strongly repulsed. They say, 'All this dancing around the witch is ghoulish. People have died and you are sick bastards.' I get both perspectives. I move between the two myself.

Sarah: So do I.

Helen: As we came into the courthouse today, there was a big crowd, a queue snaking around outside Courtroom Four.

Thirty people were jostling at the door. I couldn't get inside. They're here in force. Kelly, the dairy farmer, said how aggressive people were in the queue.

Chloe: The public gallery wants a plot twist. One woman said, 'Something big has to happen soon.'

❖

Telecommunications expert Dr Matthew Sorrell, who runs a private forensic consultancy, arrives in court.

Helen: The guy with the telephone evidence barged onto the witness stand like the cavalry riding up. He's chubby and likeable with a thick mass of very curly hair that's cut to make him look ordinary in a suit.

This does not, however, mark a change in tempo: for two days, and in granular detail, Sorrell testifies about mobile-phone data analysis generally, and Erin's mobile-phone activity specifically.

Mobile service data suggests that, on 28 April 2023, Erin had travelled to the Loch area where one of the death cap clusters had been identified on iNaturalist. A few hours later, she purchased a Sunbeam dehydrator for $229 from a Leongatha appliances store.

Sorrell tells the court that records from a phone registered to Erin showed the handset had connected consistently to a

Loch South base station for about forty-three minutes on the morning of 22 May 2023, suggesting she was in or around that location. Later that morning, her phone connected to the base station in Outtrim for twenty-five minutes. Outtrim is where Tom May had posted his death cap mushroom sighting the day before, on 21 May 2023.

In cross-examining Dr Sorrell, the defence tries to put this evidence in a different light.

'Can I suggest,' Mandy offers, 'that this set of records… is consistent with the phone never entering the Outtrim postcode? That's one explanation?'

'There are locations outside the Outtrim postcode where this set of records could conceivably come up.'

'I agree with you on that point,' says Mandy.

Chloe: The phone guy was using language that could apply to fungi. It's all about networks again.

Sarah: My God.

Chloe: 'Data connections', 'data bearer', 'dominant coverage'. Phone networks deliver messages through cells and antenna. It's the electronic version of what fungi does. Fungi is called the Wood Wide Web, isn't it? It carries messages and data and pings to each organism. Erin's been ensnared in both natural and man-made networks. Imagine the complexities of being an investigator on this case.

❖

Helen and Chloe are staying at the Nightcap. They have dinner alongside a group of other reporters, podcasters and documentary producers. A fevered, slightly competitive edge can now be felt as interest in this trial grows more intense. They wake the next morning in the motel room.

Chloe: In the middle of the night, I decided, I'm going to get up and leave a note on Helen's pillow and flee. I thought, This is ridiculous. What *are* we doing here? This is just *utterly* gross! And then, at about two o'clock, I heard you say in your sleep, 'The problem is, it's just not very interesting.' And I thought, She's thinking the same thing.

Helen: Being around those blokes was a rather deflating experience. They are so…I don't know, just so blokey.

Chloe: They are…

Helen: …incredibly, sort of, revved up.

Chloe: I noticed that nobody asked you a question.

Helen: I wouldn't expect them to. That's what happens when you get old. You're not in it. Not in it—the way those old people keep being cut out of the story.

Chloe: They're killed off again.

Helen: You can't assert yourself without being like Germaine

Greer—someone who'd elbow in full of opinions and express them loudly. Once your hearing packs up, if there's a big, rolling conversation going fast, especially when it's men, you're swept to the banks.

Chloe: It's cruel.

Helen: Ah well, you just lose your place in the stream. Must be really exhausting to be a bloke. You're on all the time. I mean that sort of bloke. They have to be the centre of everything, a bit like those diagrams the phone-data witness showed in court yesterday. They have to be the electronic base station that everything pings off.

Do you ever wish that you were a man?

Chloe: No.

Helen: No, neither do I.

Chloe: Although, having said that, I kept having these strange dreams, half-thinking, I've got to tell this to Helen. I dreamt last night that I had a penis.

Helen: Well, okay, but that's not *you* wishing you were a man.

Chloe: People were saying, 'You don't have a penis.' And I looked in the mirror naked, and I was like, 'Oh, but I do.' I also dreamt that you and I and Erin Patterson were in a bookshop together.

Helen: Wow. I just went out like a light.

Chloe: Something strange happened in the bookshop that I can't remember. And I found I didn't have a penis, after all.

Helen: Oh, you had a look, did you? It's hard to capture the spooky feeling of dreams. They're like a little jet from the unconscious that shoots up something raw. To ignore them seems to me ungrateful to your psyche.

What are we going to do about breakfast?

We get in the car and drive to Jay Dee's Cafe. We look at the menu.

Helen: I'm starting to feel that for once in our lives we are advantaged by being women, because our whole approach to this thing is deeper and more subtle. The things that vitally interest women aren't the same as the stuff those hard-charging guys care about.

Chloe: Maybe that was why I had my dream about having a penis that wasn't a penis.

Helen: It was just a phallus.

Chloe: Just attachable power.

Helen: I met a woman at a Freud conference. She told me she'd been talking with some quite highly educated people, and was amazed to find that they had never in their lives heard the term 'phallic symbol'. And, wait, have I added that they were German? *Phallische Symbole*. And she said, 'It was particularly surprising, because what I was describing was a row of carrots in a grocer's window.'

Chloe: Wait, maybe there is a connection here.

Helen: I don't know what the connection could be.

Chloe: We're going to have to delete this from the transcript, but to all those phallic-looking mushrooms.

Helen: Oh my God, here we go again. We can't get away from these bastards, the *Phallische Symbole*. That's how you pronounce it.

Amanita phalloides is specifically named for its resemblance to a phallus, particularly when the mushroom emerges from its egg-like volva. In 1727, the French botanist Sebastien Valliant labelled the mushroom *Fungus phalloides, annulatus, sordide virescens, et patulus* (a phallus-shaped, ring-stemmed, dirty green mushroom with a large spreading cap). The death cap is also known as the 'destroying angel'.

❖

Sarah arrives in Morwell after completing her other work. She meets us in Jay Dee's. We tell her about the general vibe.

Sarah: Even women's crime becomes a pissing contest for which man owns the story.

❖

The court has heard how the death cap mushrooms likely travelled from the forest or football field to Erin Patterson's kitchen. Then, in the leftovers from the fateful lunch, they made their way via police car to the Leongatha Hospital, and then, alongside Erin, by ambulance to Monash Medical Centre. There, the toxicology registrar organised for them to be sent by urgent taxi to the Royal Botanic Gardens National herbarium, where a twenty-four-hour service is run by mycologists to identify poisonous mushrooms. As the leftovers had arrived after hours, a herbarium staff member dropped the two zip-locked bags off at the home of Swiss-trained mycologist, Dr Camille Truong.

Truong had her own microscope, and she wiped down her kitchen benches, sterilised her implements, put on gloves and began tweezering out pieces of mushroom to examine them. Truong found only finely chopped supermarket field mushrooms. She rebagged the leftovers and put them in her fridge. The next day Truong took the bags back to the Royal Botanic Gardens where she looked at the chopped mushroom's morphology again with a stronger microscope, and photographed their spores. Truong then sent the leftovers for further toxicological testing. This time traces of *Amanita phalloides* were detected.

Sarah: Oh, that's a strong image of interconnectedness, the leftovers of the beef Wellington travelling those distances, passing into different hands.

Chloe: I don't think Erin saw that coming. Sometimes, as a writer, there's a detail that you don't know how to deal with, or maybe it makes you laugh—like the beef Wellington for me. But if you can look at it the right way, it's a portal into something deeper and bigger.

Sarah: It's signalling to you, 'Look again! I'm weird for a reason.'

Helen: I'm reminded of a book event I did in Canberra. The book was about a local murder, and I was amazed by the number of people who turned up. It wasn't just because of the book. It was because of the case. People got up and began speaking. It was the first time I grasped that, as a community, they were horrified, angry, stricken—*and*, I felt, they were ashamed. You can quadruple that in a community the size of this Gippsland one. The book event was full of grief and it rocked me. I had no idea that's how a small community works.

Sarah: It also raises the point that, even though Erin had been in the community for nearly twenty years, she wasn't an insider.

Chloe: That's interesting. Erin Pearson from the *Age* came

over to our table just before you arrived. The three of us have been fumbling around trying to find some meaning here, and Pearson, who's just so smart and experienced, said, 'Actually, I think that Erin Patterson is really normal. But she thought she was smarter than everybody else, and that she wouldn't get caught—that the family would be at country hospitals that weren't going to test for death cap poisoning.' Pearson imagines that Erin is probably really angry about the money and believes herself betrayed by the family. And, that in that church community, she felt like an outcast.

Sarah: It's so solid-sounding. No baroque explanation. It's hiding like a mushroom in plain sight. Maybe this is the most horrifying thing of all. That somebody who has the dark feelings we all experience, despite so many resources, still chose that path. The rest of us are just pushing it down into a ball in our stomachs.

Chloe: I have a friend whose instinct is to look away from this trial because she feels women do these sorts of things when they're backed into a corner. She hates that Erin Patterson is being treated as a witch.

Helen: The witchy thing makes no impression on me whatsoever. At no point have I been attracted to that theory even momentarily. I feel I understand her in some awful way. Anybody who's been in a broken family can understand. She has a sullen, tearful expression that gives you a creepy feeling of...*oh God*...Anyway, she was somebody for whom everything was out of control. She was quote mad unquote.

Chloe: Someone who idealises people and then demonises them as enemies.

Helen: There's an expression with certain personality disorders, that those people have to have a 'target of blame'. Maybe she narrowed her target to these people. Did she come to hate their earnestness, their goodness? She got on with her father-in-law, but he was an intellectual. The women though...

Sarah: Let's not forget her incendiary mental state at the time of the lunch. Everything was flammable. She'd just pulled both her kids out of their school and put them into another one, mid-year.

Helen: Without consulting Simon, which, to me, is an act of extreme intra-family aggression. Don't you think? Or is it not aggression but despair?

Chloe: It's aggression.

Sarah: What would real power look like? Would real power be an email to Simon, cc'ing his parents, like, 'I don't consent to the kids going to this school. Let's have a meeting with a mediator or a lawyer. Let's formalise the terms of the separation so there is a way of deciding school issues fairly.' Is that what real power looks like? It doesn't look like sneakily taking them out at the start of term three, and it doesn't look like killing everybody. This keeling—between extreme compliance and extreme aggression—suggests she didn't have any way of being the grown-up in her life. Where did all of that hot emotion leak out?

In a beautiful William Maxwell novel that I'm reading there's the line: *evil needs a choice*. Evil is an everyday thing. Erin could persist each day in her mushrooms research and planning, and kill the grandparents, or she could not.

Chloe: Evil needs a choice.

Helen: There's one other thing. Present in the court yesterday was Ian Wilkinson, the pastor, sitting in the back row.

PART IV

The Victims

Wednesday, 22 May 2025

IAN WILKINSON COMES INTO the courtroom each day. He has grey hair, glasses and an unassuming manner. He dresses in the practical style of the region's farmers, ready for Korumburra's grey weather. On his warm black vest he has a small brooch—a silver Christian fish. He listens with composure to the legal contest. Despite being Erin Patterson's uncle-in-law and pastor for nearly twenty years, he rarely exchanged more than pleasantries with her. Now, Ian and other members of Simon's family, some carefully recording details in their notebooks, hear about Erin's real feelings towards them leading up to the lunch.

Shamen Fox-Henry, a senior digital forensic officer with Victoria Police, takes the stand to give evidence about the material found on Erin's seized computer and phones. Shamen Fox-Henry's testimony stretches over four days.

Sarah: He looks like he strode out of a pulp noir novel, with his rumpled suit and moustache. He's entirely unruffled by the defence's attempts to undermine him, or the evidence. Mandy is questioning the degree to which user input was or was not required, as if all those websites were accessed independent of Erin. It's true though that Fox-Henry hadn't had that much experience with this software.

Chloe: But these tasks sound like they're pretty mechanical. Press the on switch, run the program, and the police found millions of bits of data that they tried to interpret.

The Crown introduces messages peppered with sarcastic emojis which Erin sent her Facebook friends on 6 and 7 December 2022 in their private Facebook Messenger chat:

> ErinErinErin 6 Dec 2022: Simon's dad contacted me this morning to say that he and Gail…can't adjudicate if they don't know both sides and Simon won't give his side so, he said all that he can ask is that Simon and I get together to pray for the children. This family I swear to fucking God.
>
> I said to him about 50 times yesterday that I didn't want them to adjudicate. Nobody bloody listens to me. At least I know they're a lost cause.
>
> I wonder if they've got any capacity for self-reflection at all? I mean clearly the fact that Simon refuses to talk about personal issues in part stems from the behaviour of his parents. So that's his learned behaviour. Just don't talk about this shit.
>
> ErinErinErin 6 Dec 2022: Don rang me last night to say

that he thought there was a solution to all this if Simon and I get together and try to talk and pray together and then he also said Simon had indicated there was a solution to financial issues if I withdraw the child support claim! My head nearly exploded and I was like what?? And Don goes oh sorry just ignore what I said I don't want to get involved. So anyway I sent a group message to them all last night saying the way Simon is behaving is unconscionable and asking me to withdraw the child support claim is wrong and disadvantages me and his children and how dare he etc. Don messaged to say he and Gail don't want to get involved in the financial things but just hope we will pray for the kids.

So I replied this morning saying I understand it's uncomfortable and awkward for them but I want to copy them into this stuff because Simon needs to be accountable for the decisions he is making that are hurting his children and I would hope they care about their grandchildren enough to care about what Simon is doing. That's when Don said they tried to talk to him but he refused to talk about it so they're staying out of it but want us to pray together. I'm sick of this shit I want nothing to do with them...fuck em.

ErinErinErin 7 Dec 2022: His parents sent me a message yesterday afternoon and Simon sent me one last night but I've read neither and I don't think I will. I don't want to hear it. Simon's will just be horrible and be gaslighting and abusive and it will ruin my day and his parents' will be more weasel words about not getting involved so I think I'm going to just move on. I don't need anything from any of these people. Simon's parents say they don't want to take sides but by their very action they have.

They've had Simon for tea every night for three months and never once picked up the phone to me and asked if I'm ok and need help. So that tells me their choices. Simon wants to walk away from his responsibilities too, well that's his choice. Maybe it's easier if he's not involved in even paying their school fees, meaning I can choose their school all by myself and don't have to refer to him, if he wants them to go to a private school then he can help pay for it. If he doesn't want to help pay for it then I don't have to send them there, do I? So maybe it just means I have even more freedom and about choices, a blessing in disguise.

Sarah: I was watching the family when the messages were read out, trying to make out if there was some sense that she really had been in need of help that didn't come, as the defence would have us believe. We still don't know the kind of guy Simon was as a husband or a father.

Chloe: But with a personality like Erin's, it's very difficult to know how accurate the target of her blame is. Although, you can read those messages suggesting that she pray in lots of ways, including saying in the gentlest way possible, 'Please, fuck off.'

Sarah: That line, 'does anybody in this family have the capacity for self-reflection?'

Chloe: An amazing projection, because she's got none.

❖

Sally Ann Atkinson, who has long red hair and glasses, takes the stand. An officer at the Department of Health, she had been tasked with an urgent public-health safety investigation into the source of the death cap mushrooms.

She telephoned Erin at Monash Medical Centre on the morning of 1 August. Erin had explained that she wanted to make something 'fancy', and settled on beef Wellington. She claimed to have used a mix of button mushrooms from the supermarket and dried mushrooms from an Asian grocer. Erin said she had not foraged for the mushrooms.

At 3.30 pm, Atkinson texted Erin:

> Hi Erin, Sally from the Department of Health here. I spoke with you this morning. I have left a message for you to call me but thought it might be helpful if I let you know the sort of information I wanted to discuss. I need to know what drinks were served at the lunch. I also need to know what type of shallots you purchased and if you could please give me a basic description of the packaging of the mushrooms from the Asian grocer that would be good. Approximately weight and size of the packaging. Was it partially see-through or not? And if you can think of the names of the roads you were parked on, or near when you went to the different grocery stores, then I can get officers out looking around those areas. Even a

landmark you might have remembered at the time would be helpful. Just things to think about for when I talk to you again. Thank you, Sally.

The response from Erin came at 4.08 pm:

> Hi Sally, sure I will try to get that information all to you as soon as possible. I'm just dealing with trying to manage and look after the kids in hospital here and a bit snowed under trying to manage that. I'll get this info to you as soon as I can, but I've just been in a couple of meetings with people at the hospital when you've been trying to call.

Sally's next call, at 5.22 pm, went unanswered and she did not receive a response from Erin that day. Sally called the following morning, just before 9 am, leaving a voicemail for Erin that she had further questions to ask her. Erin did not reply. So, at 9.30 am, Sally texted her:

> Good morning Erin. I left you a voice message this morning as I really do need to work on getting parts of this investigation underway as soon as possible. I understand you probably have a lot going on, so I thought I'd message with my questions so you can respond with what you do know and work on the rest. Alternatively, I am also happy to email you if you provide me with your email address if that is an easier way to type out your responses.
>
> 1. Can you please confirm that it was definitely only the one time you cooked with the dried mushrooms when you first opened them? No one else reported symptoms or issues when they consumed them?
>
> 2. Please advise what drinks were served at lunch.

3. Please confirm what kind of shallots were used in the beef Wellington. Were they spring onions or the small individual shallot-type onions please?

4. Did you possibly use your card to purchase the mushrooms and can you please check your bank statements for the shop? That would be amazingly helpful.

5. Could there possibly be any other food leftover still in the fridge? We could get council to meet your children on-site and collect for testing?

6. Can you look [at] the maps and think of the streets you parked on, or near, that would be helpful for the shops in Oakleigh, Mount Waverley or Clayton? We are urgently organising sampling to get started today.

7. Can you recall the size and type of packaging, including colour. What made you pick that brand over any others? Thanks again for your assistance and please feel free to call me back, if you prefer.

Erin did not reply.

Mid-morning, Atkinson received a call from Katrina Cripps from Child Protection Services telling her she was making enquiries about the safety of the children that day and had an appointment with Erin at 1 pm. Cripps called Atkinson during that appointment and handed the phone to Erin so Atkinson could go through her questions with her.

She noticed that Erin now changed the time and location of where she had bought the mushrooms. Atkinson sent her officers around the grocers of Oakleigh and Mount Waverley.

Nothing they found matched Erin's description of the mushrooms she claimed to have purchased.

By the time of Atkinson's search, it was too late to save Don and Gail Patterson and Heather Wilkinson. Had the doctors known earlier that foraged mushrooms were in the beef Wellingtons they could have administered the liver-protecting drug much sooner.

❖

In court, Ian Wilkinson watches CCTV footage of Erin at a petrol station en route to her son's flying lesson. He and his wife were, at this time, in hospital on the verge of organ failure.

The CCTV shows Erin entering the BP station in Caldermeade. She wears white jeans and briefly goes into the toilets, then comes out and buys some snacks.

Sarah: She's driving her son to his flying lesson, and her lunch guests are on life support. She claims at this point to have diarrhoea. Has she given herself any death-cap-laced food, or is she literally shitting herself because she is realising the consequences of what she's done?

Chloe: She was a flight-control operator, and the kid was learning to fly. What's that about? Control? Escape?

Sarah: Flight controllers require high levels of meticulousness and low emotional reactivity. You have to be able to hold the line while pilots are falling out of the sky. I was watching that big blue sky through the court window, and the cockies were wheeling. Erin's able to see that. There are cars on the road and people in the cars. Right on the other side of this pane of glass is the big world. It's even on the CCTV. If I was her watching that, I'd be like, Oh, what I wouldn't give to walk into a petrol station toilet right now. She might never get to one again.

❖

On the day the forensic pathologist is called to give evidence, Nanette Rogers turns from the bar table and discreetly warns the family members that they may prefer not to listen. Some get up and leave the courtroom. Ian stays.

The forensic pathologist, Dr Brian Beer, tells a distressing story in such a soft voice that the jury asks him to speak up: Heather died first, on 4 August at 2.05 am. Her older sister, Gail, died later that day, at 5.55 pm. Despite an emergency liver transplant, Don died on 5 August at 11.30 pm.

Death cap toxins can be difficult to identify. Traces of *Amanita phalloides* were detected in samples from Don and Ian, but not from Gail or Heather. The autopsies, however, showed the three deaths were caused by liver dysfunction and associated multi-organ failure, consistent with having ingested death caps, a poison that is particularly insidious. The body keeps recycling the toxins through the liver in an attempt to purge them. This leads to the organ's necrosis. As the liver dies, a chain reaction begins and, one by one, other organs fail. Ian was given a liver transplant and began to improve. He was discharged onto a rehabilitation ward on 11 September.

Sarah: The forensic language is dissociated, deliberately, from the hotness of life. And Beer's evidence took us back to the physicality that is the stuff of murder. Part of that horror is the necessary reduction of a human life to units of mass. We heard about the weight of Don's heart, that he was literally big-hearted.

Helen: As soon as people start talking about a heart, it's impossible not to think of all its meanings. It was a brilliant stroke by the prosecution. We talk about our emotions and other people's characters through the metaphor. Whether someone had a cold heart or a warm heart.

Chloe: Don was heavy-hearted.

Helen: Yes, and it's a human connection—we've all got a heart. It brought the whole thing very close. At a trial, you can't possibly sit there for five weeks in a state of grief, or shock, you withdraw into your intellect in order to try to comprehend what you're looking at. And then, every now and then, something will happen that'll drag you in closer—every now and then, some little detail of a person's character or nature will be mentioned, like the two women who were excited to see Erin's new pantry and wanted to look at it.

Sarah: One had brought cake and the other had brought fruit.

Helen: Yes, and Don, the old man with heart. When I heard about him right at the beginning, when Simon spoke about how Erin had always loved him and got on well with him, I had a big rush of feeling for my various fathers-in-law and remembered the tenderness that can exist in that relationship.

Sarah: Measuring someone's heart—that's what we're doing here and what I suspect a jury actually does. The reduction of a human life is also the business of the courts. If Erin is found guilty, Justice Beale is going to be translating moral culpability and harm caused into a unit of time. In this strange crucible of the courtroom, everything that is wild and overwhelming and uncertain and chaotic is reduced to numbers and units of measurement and comparability.

The jurors had also heard of the desperate struggle of surgeons and emergency physicians to keep the family members alive.

Sarah: This drawn-out fight for life—and the quiet heroism of the doctors in the face of that—was harrowing to listen to. Gail and Don and Heather didn't really have a chance.

After we heard about Don's heart, the jury stood to go

out on a break. Erin watched them leaving the room. She appeared to be in tears. Are we primed to think of this as performative? Is there a way you could cry and demonstrate your remorse that would be believable in that situation? I don't know.

Chloe: I thought Erin looked beleaguered when previously she's looked composed. She looked kind of like the demons were...

Helen: ...gnawing at her vitals.

Chloe: Yes.

Sarah: Can we talk about the difference between remorse and regret?

Helen: Raimond Gaita says that remorse is a pained, bewildered realisation of what it means to have wronged someone.

Sarah: Regret is self-interested. Remorse is a deeper thing.

Helen: I imagine that, if you're in the dock, you have to use every ounce to hold yourself together while you're being stared at by the curious people of the world. So the question would be, rather, Is she completely numb? Or is she even angry?

Could she feel that she wasn't guilty? People persuade themselves that they haven't done things, or that a whole regiment of slights or brutalities cancels out the crime.

Chloe: Sometimes she has an obstinate look.

Sarah: Wounded and wronged.

Chloe: But then there was a moment yesterday where she saw Ian Wilkinson and his daughters and I'm sure I saw her blanching. They came in after lunch and she looked over at them with an almost plaintive air. Not one of them made eye contact with her. It was like she didn't exist. Erin sat down, a lost child, trapped.

Sarah: She keeps changing. When she's following evidence on her iPad and her glasses slide midway down her nose, she does this practised flick with her scrolling finger. You can see her in her kitchen, researching, researching.

Chloe: As the doctors were describing how these three, and nearly four, people slowly suffered and died, I thought, Oh, she must be sitting there feeling horrified. But if you're a sociopath, would this be in some way gratifying? She has set this story in motion, and now gets to hear in graphic detail how her plan panned out.

The women who died did good works. Heather taught refugees English. Gail read to the blind. They were the ones in the background making cups of tea and holding everything together. And there was a moment where I could see Ian Wilkinson listening to the details of their autopsies, with Erin directly behind him. They were both in profile, and they looked like two heads on a coin. In terms of clear black-and-white stories, he'd tried to be godly and she is being tried for a triple murder.

Helen: We don't know what her tears meant, but I keep thinking of how fond Simon said Erin and his father were of each other. He said she loved his gentle nature. They both read and had some kind of intellectual connection. If she had a special feeling for him, perhaps that was what pierced her composure.

We talk on the phone to Andrew Watson, the nephew of Chloe's partner. Don Patterson had been his teacher at Korumburra High School in the late 1980s. He taught Andrew year eleven physics.

Andrew: The thing about Don was his incredible breadth of knowledge. There were four to six kids in the classroom and so we had a lot of one-on-one time with Don. We spoke about all sorts of things. Escape velocities for rocket ships. The hydraulic forces that keep tree branches up. All of the things that interested us. He could go down any rabbit hole he was asked about.

I wanted to do chemistry in year twelve, and I would have been the only student doing the subject. So I was sent to a private school. In most subjects it was like starting from scratch. I found it very difficult academically, except in physics. Even through university, the stuff that Don taught stuck with me.

Helen: What was his way of teaching that made it so striking to you?

Andrew: He drew you in. You would ask a question, and he would go up to the blackboard and just start to pull it apart and show you the equations that were relevant. It was an incredible way to explore, to look for evidence and the structure around things, and how these things could be better understood.

He would have been in his late thirties, early forties. We knew he came from Botswana, where he'd been a missionary, and us kids were always a bit suspicious about religion, but he never gave any indication of any religious affiliation in his teaching. We just knew that he had done this thing. He would talk about some of the experiences.

Chloe: What was the school like?

Andrew: Three hundred and fifty or so students in a sporty school. I would say forty per cent of kids were off farms. Academic achievement was a bunch of certificates that were handed out as people walked out the door. It was a sort of 'get yourself through' place. Of my year, only a handful went to university.

Sarah: What physical sense did you have of him?

Andrew: I can certainly remember a pair of too-tight shorts and socks under the sandals. He was very understated, red hair, a cherubic, rounded face with a dimple. He got a bit flushed, the occasional times he got angry.

Chloe: You told me at Christmas that you had planned to go and see him.

Andrew: Yeah, Mum was going to drop some stuff around at their place—Mum and Gail read the local paper for the blind. She had Don's mobile number. I had his number. It's one of those things that I just never got around to. Regretfully.

Helen: It sounds like a really happy classroom life. He must have loved you students, and been so relaxed that he could teach at full bore without having to hold back. That's such a marvellous thing.

Andrew: There's so much that I can recall from it all, to be honest. I'm an engineer: it really instilled in me a way of thinking on my feet. A way to actually look at a problem and start to pull it apart, down to its basic details, and build it back up again. I got that from him.

THE DETAILS OF Erin Patterson's story are now being reported all over the world. The number of photographers outside the court seems to have doubled. Reporters stand waiting to do live-crosses to London or New York. Two hundred and fifty-two journalists and outlets are on the court media's daily email list, including representatives from fifteen international media outlets. There are seven podcasters, seven documentary crews, one television drama series and nine authors, including us.

Details from the courtroom are being live-reported in minute-by-minute detail.

Helen: What does it mean that people want to know about this, and right away? The immediacy of it? It makes me feel very twitchy.

Sarah: Is there something in the fact that it is such a domestic crime? Most people have a kitchen and family they could invite over for lunch. A lot of violent crimes have some distancing factor that presents like a horror movie. This one is a more intimate horror.

Chloe: The *Guardian* court reporter Nino Bucci said he goes from here to the inquest into the death of Kumanjayi Walker, who was shot by police in the Northern Territory. The *Guardian* is sending him even though the readership for that story is minuscule. People are just not clicking on it, but they can't get enough of what feels, at least from the outside, like a *Midsomer Murders* episode. It's comfortably middle class and white. There's not the discomfort of racism or horrendous poverty.

Helen: Well, it 'could be us'.

Chloe: Most people don't just have family, they also have some in-law or relative with whom there's tension or feuding…

Helen: …or long-standing, unexpressed rage.

Sarah: Statistically, you're more likely to be killed by someone you know. We see the sickening regularity of women being killed by their partners. But this is that statistic represented in an exceptional way: it's familiar *and* unexpected. You get the titillating thrill of just how terrible it is.

Chloe: The other day, Sarah described one cohort in the

courtroom as the Real Housewives of Morwell. Then yesterday, a woman leaned over to me and said of Helen's friend, Kelly, the dairy farmer, 'She thinks she's the boss of the court.' Kelly had stood up to get some tissues off the bar table and was blowing her nose. And the woman next to me could see that Erin had a jug of water and paper cups over at the dock. She wanted to go and pour herself a drink.

Helen: All this in the absence of the judge and jury, right?

Chloe: Yeah, it was just people who had taken the day off work and settled in.

Helen: What about that dude who looks like one of the guys who broke into the US Capitol? He's wearing rabbit fur in rainbow colours.

Chloe: Also, everyone has a notebook.

Helen: They're true-crime influencers.

Chloe: At lunch yesterday, one of the journalists came into the cafe. He realised that Erin's power of attorney was sitting by herself. Suddenly we were in an aquarium, watching a shark slowly make a line to the table next to hers—which was also the table next to ours. He introduced himself, saying, 'Look, I can really see how this has affected Erin *horribly*,' and asked whether Erin might not like to speak to him? And the POA said, 'Look, Erin is a very private person.' But he was warming her up. By the end she told him his newspaper was the only one she subscribed to, and added, 'You know, I'm a trained social worker, advocating for people is my jam.'

Sarah: Remember when she told Helen she had mistaken her for a 'CWA busybody'? She apologised. I was chatting with her the other day about how we've been here so much we haven't been able to get haircuts. And she said, 'I promised Erin I won't get my greys touched up until she can.'

Chloe: Of all the huge stories happening in the world, why are we all here? Climate change, the Middle East, AI about to take our jobs, the threat to democracy. But that is *exactly* why everyone is here. So as *not* to think about these things.

Helen: The poor family. Yesterday, we were all going out of the court together and I held the door open for Ian Wilkinson. His manner was, Thank you, somebody's being polite to me.

Chloe: We've also engaged at the door. The court is so small. He held the door open for me, and turned with a quiet smile, as if to say, This is a communal thing that we do for each other…

Helen: …that still shows some bond of goodness.

Tuesday, 27 May 2025

As rain pelts the windowpane on the twentieth day of the trial, the Crown calls its final witness, Detective Leading Senior Constable Stephen Eppingstall. The tall, broad, police officer has sat silent in the court for the last five weeks. Now, as though he can't bear to sit any longer, he stands to give his evidence. Eppingstall has been a member of the police force for twenty years, nearly fifteen of them as a detective. He had initially believed the deaths would be a coronial matter. After a couple of weeks, he changed his mind and felt the case needed to be investigated as a homicide. As he put it in the pre-trial hearing, 'When we started getting into the computer material, that's when my personal opinion of it changed and we went down this path.'

He stands with his feet spread in their heavy-soled boots, wearing a grey suit and glasses. He appears nervously polite, answering all the Crown's questions with 'Yes, ma'am' or 'No, ma'am'. He keeps his hands steady by locking his thumbs and making a gun shape with his fingers.

Eppingstall tells the jury that the police think Erin used three mobile phones. Their SIM cards had been repeatedly swapped. On 5 August, while the police were executing a search warrant at Erin's home, she handed over one mobile, which was later discovered to have been wiped and returned to its factory settings several times in the days after the lunch. It was even reset during the police search when Erin was briefly left alone to call a lawyer. This phone was also remotely wiped while it was in a locker at the Wonthaggi police station.

The mood in the courtroom changes.

Sarah: Everyone seems to have reached a tipping point of exhaustion. There's a lot of laughter about silly things.

Helen: Even the bereaved people laughed, even Ian Wilkinson. Everybody is so tired that I think their inhibitions are loosened up. In courts, there's a kind of overwhelming solemnity for a while. If somebody says something that's funny, it's a bit like laughing in church. And yet today people freely laughed. There was more eye contact between the people in the room. It was much more human. The policeman kept saying, 'Yes, ma'am. Yes, ma'am, yes. No, ma'am. Yes, ma'am.' And the judge suddenly burst out, 'Stop saying, ma'am, you don't need to say ma'am.' And everyone laughed and Eppingstall said, 'I used to be in the army. It's really hard to break a habit.' We all laughed sympathetically. And when he was asked the next question, he stood up really straight, like a boy who'd been hauled over the coals, and just said, 'Yes'. The whole court cracked up.

We are sitting at a table in a small Morwell shopping centre eating pies from Out of Dough.

Sarah: There's a butcher and a baker, no candlestick maker, sadly. But there is a liquor shop.

Helen: This is sort of daggy. It makes me feel at home. Look at that green bucket sitting there with the price tag still on it.

The court was shown a video of the homicide detectives sitting opposite Erin at her kitchen table, taking possession of the phone.

Sarah: We briefly heard Erin's voice on this recorded tape, and I think it was the first time we've heard her speak in the courtroom. We saw inside her house, inside her kitchen.

I think the kids were at home, so the police were very careful to make this search as administrative a procedure as possible. But, you know, there was the *RecipeTin Eats* cookbook on the counter with its food-spattered beef Wellington recipe on page 252. There was the walk-in pantry that Heather and Gail had been excited to have a look at.

Helen: It was brand-new looking. Everything was white,

freshly painted. The furnishings were grey and beige, and there was a blonde wood floor, but there was also a feeling that it hadn't been lived in all that much yet. And finally, the pantry that the old ladies, God bless them, were terribly interested in, because Heather was getting a pantry. A pantry is a big deal for that generation. But the pantry looked kind of bleak and a bit sad.

Sarah: All the spaces were notably clutter-free. Remember, she'd been there for a year. All the usual detritus of life seemed to be missing from the benchtops and the walls and the shelves and even inside the drawers. It was almost like one of those display houses that are not lived in at all.

Chloe: We saw footage of Erin sitting at the table where she'd served this lunch. That was a strange moment in the courtroom: Ian Wilkinson, who survived the meal, was suddenly plunged back to that table, and so was Erin. She's been in jail for eighteen months—this is not the homecoming she would have hoped for.

Sarah: The house was frozen in time.

Chloe: Talking of how domestic this story is, here we are looking inside this woman's dishwasher. Inside her crockery cupboards. Inside all the drawers. Because, of course, they're trying to prove that the grey plates, on which she served the poisonous meals, have gone missing. It was very, very, very domestic.

Helen: Well, looking into a woman's kitchen—if you didn't want anyone to know you, you wouldn't ask them into your kitchen, would you. I found the kitchen kind of heartbreaking, like everything else in this story. It was as though she hadn't had a chance to live in it yet, but now it's too late. She's already done the thing that's made it impossible.

If you own more than one house, you've got boltholes…

Chloe: …unlike a lot of women who are stuck in relationships that have broken down. She had the means to find a different way to live.

Helen: But when you look at that kitchen, you see she's run out of track. There's no way forward. What she's done means there's a screech of brakes. She's run out of fantasy.

Chloe: But she hasn't run out of track, because it continues in this courtroom. She's sitting in the dock thinking there's a chance she'll be acquitted.

❖

After lunch, the video of the police record of interview is played in court. It has the typically strange angles of procedural filming. In the box-like interview room, Erin's profile looms in the foreground. Two homicide detectives are little more than voices. Erin tells them that she couldn't stay at the hospital to receive the recommended treatment for death cap poisoning because she first had to go home to feed her animals and pack her daughter's ballet bag.

Afterwards, Sarah and Chloe return with Helen to the Nightcap motel. It's late afternoon, getting dark, some rain is coming, and we're all in Helen's room.

Chloe: We've been puzzling over Erin for weeks. I found seeing her on screen, while she was right behind us, surreal. What did you think?

Sarah: On the one hand, she was small and scared. Even saying her age—she was forty-eight—and speaking in this little-girl voice. And then—this was like an electric shock—very early in the questioning, she gets highly annoyed. When the detective asks whether she's an Australian citizen. She snaps at him.

Helen: 'I was born in Australia. I've lived my whole life in Australia.'

Chloe: When the detectives tell her that her mother-in-law and her mother-in-law's sister have just passed away, she appears strangely pissed off. She's on her high horse—she says she has already helped the health authorities by answering all their questions, which we know is not true.

Helen: She also told a rather big lie in the first few minutes of the interview—when they asked if she had a dehydrator, she said she'd never had a dehydrator.

Chloe: The police had already found the footage of her taking it to the tip. They'd also opened her kitchen drawer and found the dehydrator's instruction manual.

Sarah: Showing up at hospital clearly didn't go how Erin thought it would. Why did she discharge herself after five minutes? Why did she resist medical treatment for herself and her kids? Her answers made no sense, and nothing answered Eppingstall's key question: Four people who were at the lunch are gravely ill and we're interested in why you are not.

Chloe: She reminded me of a child telling lies. She had a self-pitying tone in the video. And meanwhile, behind us in court, she was absolutely bawling. She was as upset as I've seen her. There was a telling remark she made in that interview, that her mother-in-law and father-in-law had said, 'they would always support me emotionally. And I appreciated that.' But the messages to her Facebook friends contradict this. She was angry with them for supporting Simon over her. In the police interview, she said, 'Simon hates that I still have this relationship with them, that they still love me.' It felt like she was rivalrous, prosecuting the case even as they were dead or dying. Her animus was sporing up from the undergrowth.

Sarah: Like, I'll take them away from you, even though they mean this much to me. Or maybe they didn't mean that much to her.

Helen: She also spoke about how both her parents were dead, and that she had no family.

I still feel she thought it was going to save her, to marry into this stable family, and that's why she was so angry with them. We don't really know what went wrong in the marriage, but we learned from the messages she sent that she felt awfully let down by them—even betrayed.

Chloe: Seeing her in the interview, she lies very easily.

Helen: Yep, naturally slides into it…

Sarah: …with authority.

It's been raining. The view from the big window was totally obscured by fog. It just rolled in and swallowed up the mountains we've looked out at over the last few weeks. As soon as Erin started speaking in the video, I was like, Okay, now we're going to get some insight. But the view I'd had of her was also swallowed up, and I was no closer to clarity. The intellect is there. But the feeling you'd expect isn't. She bounces between smallness and grandiosity. I'm even more confused.

Helen: Me too. We talked at lunchtime about the strange intimacy of being able to see inside a woman's house, particularly her kitchen, and how little you could tell from hers. The kitchen was like a terrible roadblock. The big ending happened there.

Chloe: Watching her today, I thought, Oh, you're nuts!

Helen: Did you?

Chloe: Oh, you're *totally*—

Helen: —crazy, is that what you mean?

Chloe: I'm not sure crazy is more sensitive than nuts. But here is someone who has a significant disorder.

Sarah: Yes, but she won't be treated as insane for legal purposes.

Chloe: I understand she was walking around leading a normal-seeming life, but I think if we were in close quarters with her, speaking to her for a long time, we'd pick up that there was a problem.

Sarah: Whatever we want to call it, disorder seems to be in the courtroom with us, and we are feeling it as well.

Chloe: We walk in each morning and people seem almost excited. There's this naive expectation: maybe today we're going to find out the truth. Then, within five minutes, confusion blankets the whole room. Mandy is doing whatever he can to unpick and fray the prosecution story…

Sarah: …and the story isn't even the story. The shadow case—her attempts to kill Simon—is not allowed into the room. It's edited out according to the rules of evidence. We just get a legal narrative, the best the Crown can do within those constraints.

Helen: We're in this fog, a choking fog of not being able to understand why she did it.

Chloe: You do have to be disturbed to go and source death cap mushrooms, dehydrate them and serve them to…

Helen: …people whom you have loved and who've loved you…

Chloe: …and who love your children.

Helen: Something I've learnt from watching trials in family stories of murder—just because you love someone doesn't mean you don't ever want to kill them.

Sarah: You're still not justified in poisoning someone you hate. Forget about love. You still can't do it.

Chloe: Even the way that she behaved after the murderous lunch is unhinged.

Sarah: And again, there's this keeling between deep premeditation and…

Chloe: …no plan at all.

Sarah: Why didn't she smash that dehydrator into a million pieces and bury each shard in the bush? The police have the leftovers and the doctors have empirical data about her blood pressure and her heart rate—a perfect picture of stress at the exact moment of crisis. It must be one of the worst own goals in history, and it exists alongside this meticulous, calculated planning. Bigness and smallness.

❖

Sarah and Chloe leave Helen at the Nightcap and drive back to Melbourne. Chloe wonders why she finds Erin more disturbed than Sarah and Helen seem to.

Sarah: The money is maybe distorting it, the class is maybe distorting it, because…

Chloe: …she's well spoken.

Sarah: She's well spoken. She has a beautiful house. She has a property portfolio and she has the after-school activities and the hobby farm, and she moves at a certain altitude. Plus, she's clearly intelligent, and apparently has a sense of humour. It's like she could be…

Chloe: …somebody we know.

Sarah: Exactly. And I think if you stripped all that away, we might see, or be willing to see more clearly, the madness or the disjunct.

Chloe: There's one line that stuck out to me in the police interview. It's so minor, but while explaining her love for and connection to her in-laws, Erin said, 'I don't have parents. My sister's estranged. My grandparents are all gone.' And I thought, You're forty-eight, that's a bit old to feel orphaned by a lack of grandparents. Isn't that something that a kid might think?

Sarah: 'My grandparents are all gone.'

Chloe: Children commonly have grandparents. So are you envious that *your* children have grandparents?

Sarah: Oh, my God. Is she jealous of the children and the love that was shown to them by their father and grandparents? Because if you're not gonna love Erin, you're not gonna love…

Chloe: …anyone.

Wednesday, 28 May 2025

Eppingstall is in the witness box again. The prosecution leads him as he gives evidence about finding an entry in Gail's diary for 28 June 2023: 'Erin—St Vincent's arm lump'. He is asked to read out messages found on Gail Patterson's mobile phone.

28 June 2023 at 7.30 pm:

> Hi Erin, just wondering how you got on at your appointment today? Love Gail and Don.

Eppingstall says St Vincent's Hospital had no appointments for Erin that day.

From Erin to Gail, on 29 June 2023 at 11.52 am:

> Hi Gail, Sorry I had taken [her daughter] to see a movie last night. We saw The Little Mermaid. The appointment went ok. Thanks for asking. I had a needle biopsy taken of the lump and I'm returning for an MRI next week and we'll know more after the results of those two things.

'Did you find any evidence in the accused's medical records of her having had a needle biopsy of a lump?'

'No.'

'Did you find any evidence in the accused's medical records of her being referred for, or scheduled, or having an MRI?'

'No.'

Eppingstall is then asked to read out the reply from Gail on 29 June 2023 at 6.26 pm:

> That's a test of patience isn't it? Praying you'll know God's peace. We're just ready to relax after an enjoyable day. Nice to have the fire warming us in this cold weather xo.

Then, another message from Gail to Erin on 6 July 2023 at 8.15 pm:

> Hi Erin, how did you get on yesterday with your medical test? Love Don and Gail.

And Erin's reply on 7 July 2023 at 6.46 pm:

> Thanks for your message, Don and Gail. There's a bit to digest with everything that's come out of it all. I might talk more about it with you both when I see you in person. Love, Erin.

The Victorian Cancer Registry has no record of Erin ever having received a cancer diagnosis.

❖

After court, we're once again in Helen's room at the Nightcap, comparing notes, spinning on the same questions.

Sarah: We saw photos of Erin's home office. It was this sparse, empty-feeling room. I didn't see a single book on the shelves. Only completed Lego projects.

Chloe: Transformer-type creations. Robotic warrior figures ready for battle. There was also a lot of electronic equipment.

Sarah: It was like her life had not been unpacked. She was not really inhabiting the dream home. Her life was online. It was a fantasy life, googling the illnesses that she was scared of having, researching true crimes and with the grandiose thought: I have these poisons at my disposal to end my enemies with.

Helen: We heard in evidence an enormous list of complaints Erin had taken to her doctor, all the things that she thought were wrong with her. There were about twenty-five or thirty of them. Imagine being married to somebody who had that kind of list? She texted it to Simon. His response was, 'Holy crap, that must make it hard to live a life.'

Sarah: We've heard endlessly about Erin's diarrhoea. We've heard about her continually buying diet books on Booktopia. All her texts. Not that she's entitled to privacy by this point, but being in that courtroom with your rib cage open is appalling.

Chloe: I don't know where this woman would fit in the

diagnostic manual—what page or pages you'd open—but she felt she wasn't given the regard that was due. And it's an amazing irony that now people are fighting to get into a courtroom to see her and hear her story. She's set in motion this grand project of being regarded in minute detail.

❖

Chloe: When I pulled up this morning, the blonde reporter in the powder-blue coat was coming out of the motel that apparently has blood on the walls. The jolt seeing her stepping matter-of-factly from the house of horrors to get to work.

Helen: That's where there was a dead body in the street, isn't it?

Sarah: The hit and run? Only a few days ago, I had a thought that an accident was going to happen right there. It's a blind corner, near the rose garden.

Chloe: Well, we're just watching the sun go down…

Sarah: …over the sports bar car park.

Helen: I do really like it here. I've grown quite fond of it. I went to the bar the other night to get a little toastie. The place was empty except for a stream of blokes walking purposefully one by one through the main bar, heading for another room at the back where there was loud music and whooping and yelling. This morning someone told me it was Kevin Bloody Wilson.

Sarah: Who?

Chloe: He's a comedian and a singer.

Helen: His songs are really rude. There's one called 'D. I. L. L. I. G. A. F.' It stands for Do I Look Like I Give a Fuck? He can really sell out in Gippsland, apparently.

The Crown case is nearly over. Mandy has not yet indicated whether the defence will put its own case and call witnesses.

Chloe: There's a feeling growing that Erin is going to take the stand.

Sarah: As in, Let me get up there and talk my way out of this? I don't think that would be a tactically sound thing to do. The danger is that she will look mercenary and performative, and—especially during cross-examination—other parts of her personality that the jury will read as unpalatable will all be on display.

Chloe: What else have they got? It's the last roll of the dice, and if, aged fifty, you're about to go to jail for thirty years, then you're going to have a crack, aren't you?

Helen: What demeanour would soften the hearts of a jury in this case? Wild sobbing would not do it.

Chloe: I don't know, but if you sow enough doubt, is it possible that the jury might say, 'I don't want to separate the children from their mother'? Everybody at home following this case who thinks, 'Aha, she did it,' they're not the ones faced with a rupture that could be for the rest of those kids' lives.

Helen: In that police interview where they asked her the question that everyone gets asked—'Are you an Australian citizen?'—why did she respond as if somebody had insulted her?

Chloe: Insulted her intelligence, I thought.

Helen: But also her sense that she is a worthy person who totally belongs in this place. I don't know what it really meant that she took that tone.

Sarah: It was so incontinent. She is not in any position to snap at the detectives who have just brought her in for questioning. It's a supremely bad idea to lose control over her hostility towards this man, whom she speaks to as if she thinks he's an oaf. She's been in this room for three seconds and already she looks like an arsehole.

Helen: But when he asked her that question—'Are you an Australian?'—it pressed some button in her. What was that button?

Sarah: Maybe it was, 'You don't belong'. You don't belong

with the Baptist family. You don't belong in your family of origin. There's no place on Earth for you, and you don't belong.

Helen: I thought she was laying it on with a trowel. It was one of her spiels—I am poor, lovelorn, unloved. She's building this persona of herself as a lost soul.

Maybe it's not a persona. She *is* a lost soul.

I'm thinking, too, about Don and Gail. There was some deal that she believed had been done. She felt owed certain things by her parents-in-law, and when they stopped providing them, perhaps out of loyalty to their son, she was enraged. There's a hell of a lot of anger in those messages that she sent to the chat-group women. She felt ripped off and that justified her anger. I think she was furious that they wouldn't listen to her complaints. And they held back. They stood firm: you've just got to pray it away.

Chloe: You could feel Gail trying to placate Erin.

But I had a really strong reaction to seeing Erin in that police interview, as though the curtain had been pulled back and we'd glimpsed the little person cycling. When we were in court watching it—I'm embarrassed by this—there was a moment where I had to suppress a laugh. I felt that the joke was on us—we thought we were going to get Medea and it was actually Karen.

It's a Hannah Arendt rip-off, but the phrase that came to

me was 'the banality of sociopathy'—what's left is just this horrible damage she's wrought. In the court we're sitting among the people whose lives she completely bombed apart.

Then, last night I went out to dinner, and the host took out her phone and read a text she had from one of Simon's relatives. It was dated August 2023.

Helen: A few weeks after the lunch?

Chloe: Yeah. It was basically saying that Simon had had an amicable relationship with his estranged wife until he'd been so sick he had to be put into an induced coma, and it slowly dawned on him that she might be poisoning him. He stopped eating any food that she prepared, and he got better. But then she pretended to have cancer and invited his parents and the Wilkinsons over because Ian had had a lot of experience, through the church, of talking with children about difficult things. By mid-August—the time of this text—the family were all convinced she was a psychopath. They were terrified of what she might do next.

Helen: They were a family of decency and stability and goodwill, the whole Baptist thing. It's a big spread to include the Wilkinsons when you think she was actually furious with her parents-in-law.

Sarah: If it was sociopathy, they could have been collateral. To lure Simon there, and to make it look less intentional, to look…

Helen: …like a little lunch party.

Chloe: I don't understand a world where, after Simon has been repeatedly poisoned, everyone's excited to go over and have lunch at her house. I live in a world of more paranoia.

Helen: Or good sense.

Sarah: Perhaps it didn't occur to them that she could have any other target except for Simon.

Helen: Wait a minute. Let's cast back to the idea that, when Simon had part of his bowel removed, maybe nobody really believed that he was poisoned. I mean, if the whole family believed that she'd poisoned him, they would have gone to the police, surely…

❖

Had Erin also been tried for attempting to murder Simon, the jury would have been told a very different tale. This is the shadow story.

Simon, who was otherwise healthy, was hospitalised four times during 2021 and 2022. At the pre-trial hearing, the Crown explained that, each time, it was after eating food prepared for him by Erin.

On 16 November 2021 Erin went to Simon's place to help him pack for a trip she had suggested they take, without the children, to Wilsons Promontory. She brought him a container of penne Bolognese for his dinner, and called him that evening, encouraging him to eat it. The next day, Simon was sick. He vomited, but decided 'to try and push on', putting the nausea down to nerves at 'going away together for the first time in many years'.

In their Airbnb, while his vomiting and diarrhoea became more severe, Erin was 'reading on her phone, watching TV, relaxing'. Although she made him electrolyte drinks, his condition worsened. He wanted to go to hospital, but she thought they should just wait it out. After his repeated requests for medical help, she relented. He spent five days in Monash Medical Centre. No cause was found.

Simon recovered, and at the start of 2022 Erin suggested a camping trip. Simon joked to her that she 'might put something in my food and poison me'. They drove four hours to Howqua in the Victorian High Country.

Simon set up the tent and got the fire going. Erin cooked them a chicken korma curry with rice. Around midnight, Simon woke feeling overheated and nauseous, and began to vomit and have diarrhoea. Within days he was back at Monash Medical Centre. Erin, as his next of kin, gave medical permission for life-saving surgery, and a portion of his bowel was removed. He was in an induced coma for several days. Simon found Erin supportive and caring but he was struck by her extensive contact with his friends about his illness. Again, the doctors were unable to find a cause.

During his convalescence Erin cared for Simon in the Leongatha house they had designed together. One day she 'specially made some stew' for him, which he 'appreciated'. But once again, an attack of vomiting and diarrhoea. At 1 am they called Simon's parents, who took him to Leongatha Hospital, while Erin stayed with their sleeping children. Simon was put on a drip and given anti-nausea medication, then transported to Monash Medical Centre. After discharge he returned to Erin's house. He stayed for several weeks, but felt from her 'an increasing cold shoulder', and moved out to stay with Don and Gail.

Dr Christopher Ford, Simon's GP and Bible study partner, suggested Simon draft a spreadsheet of what had occurred. 'My thought,' said Simon in court, 'was that it could appear to someone looking at this that Erin was a cause, because of her cooking.' Still he didn't seriously entertain the prospect.

In September 2022, Simon and Erin went on a daytrip to Wilsons Prom. On a bushwalk, they passed an old graveyard. They saw a snake. They returned to the car, and Simon ate a curry and vegetable wrap that Erin had prepared. Within hours he was in an ambulance. 'By the end of the journey all I could move was my neck, my tongue and my lips.'

This time, while he was recovering, his cousin Tim Patterson called. Tim raised his suspicion—which he claimed other family members shared—that Erin could be poisoning Simon. This was the first time Simon took it seriously. He went back to Dr Ford and confided in him. Ford told Simon that if he had another unexplained medical emergency, he himself would try to ensure that toxicological testing was undertaken. Ford did not alert authorities.

Simon changed his power of attorney into his father's and brother's names, and told certain family members why.

On his 2022 tax return Simon specified his marital status as separated. After that he began to sense an increasing chill from Erin. In November 2022 she filed for child support. The former couple now barely spoke.

In February 2023, Erin came to his house with a batch of cookies she said their daughter had baked for him. She called several times to ask whether he had eaten them. He suspected they contained antifreeze, and threw them out.

That month Simon told his brother Matthew, a Baptist minister, his fears about Erin. Matthew said he thought the reason for this chronic vomiting and diarrhoea was probably Simon's 'anxiety'. He saw Simon's suspicion of Erin as 'a fairly private matter'.

In July 2023, the evening before the fatal lunch, Simon's sister Anna told her father she was worried about them eating food Erin prepared. Don brushed her concerns aside. 'No,' he said, 'we'll be okay.' Simon told his parents he wouldn't be coming to the lunch. Gail asked him why. Not wanting to worry his mother, Simon said, 'Oh, it's because of all the things that have happened in the recent past with Erin. I don't think I would be wise to go.' His father helped move the conversation past that question. In court, remembering this moment, Simon wept. His father had been 'very thoughtful'. He said, 'I suggest you don't tell too many people about this.'

The old teacher could pull apart any difficult physics problem and find a solution, but he had loved his daughter-in-law, and she was a problem that he could not solve.

❖

Sitting in Helen's motel room, we don't yet know this shadow story. Instead, we go round and round, trying to grapple with who the accused woman really is.

Sarah: I think it's as Helen said the first day, you expect to see a monster and what you see is a broken person.

Chloe: What if we expected a broken person and we're seeing a monster?

PART V

The Accused

Monday, 2 June 2025

WHEN NANETTE ROGERS CLOSED the Crown case, Colin Mandy stood up. 'Your Honour, the defence will call Erin Patterson.'

Helen: Nobody knew it was going to happen. When it was announced that she would take the stand, there was a loud gasp. People cried out. At last, at last! The judge called a break of fifteen minutes so everyone could get their shit together. I saw a spot on the bench just inside the door of the courtroom, where you can hear but you can't see anything. I lowered my arse onto it, and the woman next to me said, 'Oh no, my sister's going to sit there.' So I pushed further in and found the very last spot and grabbed it. I couldn't see the jury, except for one old man at the end of the back row. But I thought, I'm not moving again. And I'm glad I didn't, because the tipstaff was really throwing his weight around.

There was a kind of tension in the room, and I was over

on one side, so I didn't see her being brought out of the dock. But all of a sudden, boom, there she was just sitting there in the witness box. Everybody was straining at their own leash not to turn and stare. The drawing of her that they run in the newspaper is brutal. It makes her look villainous. Actually, she looks small. She was sitting there quietly, she was self-possessed, while everyone else in the room was breathless. We'd been hanging out for her to step into the limelight.

Sarah and Chloe watched Erin on a big screen in a Melbourne Supreme Court media room. Now we're on the phone together.

Sarah: What was it like?

Helen: At first I felt impressed by her. She struck me as an educated woman, well and calmly spoken, somebody who was composed. She seemed a very familiar type of person, and she was dealt with very delicately by her counsel. I bet his junior, a young woman with an obviously first-rate mind, had a lot to do with that. He was asking her things like, 'How did you feel about yourself around the time leading up to the lunch?' *How did you feel about yourself?* That doesn't sound like a man's question to me. Erin answered slowly and thoughtfully. To me, she's mysterious, even though, on one level, she is recognisable. I could imagine talking with her, having an interesting conversation. She seemed like a person of seriousness and intelligence, and yet, at the same time, she was depicting her marriage and her life in a way that was so familiar I sort of couldn't get near it. It's hard to describe this. I think a lot of people in the room were having very complex feelings. When we came out, we were all exhausted. The tension of being there and listening to her speak was almost unbearable. It's just that everyone longs to know what's inside her head.

Sarah: Did you find yourself at any point getting angry?

Helen: No, not at all. No. This was the time that I felt the most for her. I want to say something else about the way she told her life story. It was a standard modern story of a marriage that wasn't very good. There was a lot of restlessness and unhappiness in it, in her, and she gave an account of it that was almost generic. I thought, God, just about everyone I know could tell that story. *I* could tell that story. She sighed a lot. She sighed the sort of sighs that you give when someone asks you a question you've already answered, and you're thinking, Do I really have to go through this again? Can I really drag this out of myself once more?

She had a special way of talking. She spoke with a conversational tone and volume, as if she was talking to us and it was going to be a conversation. She wasn't grandly stating things, and she wasn't milking it for drama. She spoke quite bluntly about herself—not moral things or ethical things—physical things, you know, her unhappiness at having put on a lot of weight and how she decided she was going to have gastric-band surgery. And she had these little head movements that went with what she was saying. When she was serious, she would nod and then shake her head. Now that I'm talking about it, I'm starting to think that it was a very, very skilful performance. And yet I never felt that she was laying it on. It was a mysterious day and rather upsetting.

Chloe: We could see you in the courtroom with all the family sitting behind you.

Helen: She spoke lovingly about her mother-in-law. With her first baby, she had a very traumatic and difficult birth, a great suffering for her and for the baby. At this point Erin and Simon were living in Western Australia. Don and Gail came to stay with them to help with the baby. Mr Mandy asked her, 'And how did you feel about having them there in the house?' She said, 'I was really glad they were there. Gail was very patient and gentle with me. She taught me how to interpret his cries.' I thought that was a beautiful expression—to interpret his cries. Gail had earned her trust.

Chloe: But not knowing how to interpret other people's needs or pain—that's striking, isn't it?

Helen: When she said that, I glanced up at the jury. The only one of them I could see was breathing fast, the lines on his face seemed to get deeper. I thought, He's either about to have a heart attack, poor fellow, or he's almost crying listening to her.

The marriage went pear-shaped pretty early on. They'd been living in Perth but, when the baby was only a few months old, they went on a huge trip, taking the baby, around Australia in a Nissan Patrol. She said twice, 'We came down through the guts' of the country. I got the impression that she enjoyed travelling, but that she got sick of it after a while and wanted to stop. She said, 'I wanted to have babies, but he wanted to keep travelling.'

Simon had previously testified that Erin had left him and the baby in Townsville and flown home. Simon drove, with their son, the 4000 kilometres back to Perth. This was their first separation. Erin lived with the baby in a small cottage while Simon lived in a caravan nearby. They had some sessions of marriage counselling, and reunited.

Erin said the biggest issue in their marriage was poor communication.

Sarah: Her story is a legal instrument. It's impression management; its purpose is to sway the jury. So it's highly selective. It's a perfectly serviceable tale about 'our early life'.

But then you start looking at it, and it's full of holes.

This upwelling of emotion around the love she felt for her mother-in-law, as if she couldn't have killed her, when everything else that we're learning seems to show the love that she once felt for them is the reason she killed them. She has this hypersensitivity about not belonging, not being included. She can't stay in one place for any sustained period of time, not in any job or study or relationship. She can't persist in any one thing despite having every resource, intellectual and financial, at her disposal. And so, yeah, I was very suspicious of that. She does this thing where every so often she'll pause and her eyes will flare. There's just too much of the whites around her eyes. And this jutting forward of her head. It's like this wall of energy with these flared eyes. It's unsettling. Watching her so closely today, on that huge screen in the Supreme Court media room, I noticed that the first time she responded—when Mandy asked her age—with 'Fifty', her eyes flared and Mandy faltered slightly. There's some force sheeting off her. There is something there that I did not expect after sitting in the same room as her all these weeks.

Chloe: Her love story is also a horror story. It was moving being catapulted back to a part of her life that was sweet: Erin described becoming friends with Simon and his group of friends and going camping with them most weekends, and them slowly getting to know each other. She was trying to convert him to atheism, and then one weekend Simon took her to his uncle's church. And hanging in the church there was a banner that read, 'Faith, Hope and Love'. Ian was giving a sermon on love, quoting St John. 'God is love and he who abides in love abides in God and God abides in him.' And then Erin was offered communion. She claims the service had a profound impact on her.

> I had what at best can be described as, like a spiritual experience. I'd been approaching religion as an intellectual exercise up until that point. Does that make sense? Is it rational? But I had what I would call a religious experience there and it quite overwhelmed me.

Chloe: Presumably Don and Gail, her future parents-in-law, were present that day, along with Ian and Heather.

Erin's spiritual experience is a key moment in the love story. But then, there's the horror story, especially if you're a family member now watching the woman who came into your church and your family and allegedly poisoned it.

Sarah: It's devastating. Every point in the story has that duality.

Chloe: Something's always underneath.

Sarah: For me, the most difficult thing today was when she was talking about the house that they had built, and she said, 'I saw it as my final house.' The final house—where the children would grow up and where they could come back and stay however long they want and bring their children. And then she said, 'And I would grow old there, or so I thought.' Now it's a crime scene.

Chloe: People talk about a 'forever home', but this was the final house for her parents-in-law, who were having the kind of life she supposedly pictured for herself.

Sarah: We talked in our earliest conversations about what it actually means to abide. What adaptations and sacrifices you have to make in order to abide for the long haul in any situation or relationship.

Erin was estranged from her parents, so Don and Gail became even more important for the practical and emotional support they gave. Love betrayed is often the motive for extreme rage. I almost find it more incriminating the more she talks about this well of deep feeling she had for them, because this rage about rejection hovers at the edges.

Helen: I felt awful when it was over today. I was sad. I thought it was an archetypal modern story of marriage not being something that people are up to anymore. I thought, she's sat down with her counsel and shaped this story. But then I felt that familiar sadness of when you're fucking something up in a really big way.

Sarah: Well, I think this accounts for why people are so gripped by this. It's a very recognisable, unexplosive-until-the-end narrative of the domestic and the everyday.

It made me think of how she had described her childhood so darkly and what it might have meant to her to step into that little church and find herself welcomed. That in itself could've felt like a spiritual experience.

Chloe: It must have been heightened: love and at the same time God. Those two feelings of heat commingling. Although, interestingly, Sarah and I noted that Erin didn't take an oath on the Bible. She made an affirmation today.

Hearing her story about being in the church, I thought, she is a Krasnostein character, like someone in Sarah's book *The Believer*.

Sarah: Oh, that's interesting. Yeah, in that book I was really interested in the too-perfect stories people tell themselves when they can't face the gap between the world as it is and the world as they desperately wish it would be. There's a chance that her spiritual experience was just another easy lie. But maybe it wasn't: she sounds like she was ravenous. Family-hungry. Acceptance-hungry.

But it's not hanging together. I wonder if we're going to get a sense of the core, the true self, in Erin. I can see, as Helen said, these glimpses—the funny person, the clever person, the friend, the wife, the mother, the daughter-in-law, the child—but I don't trust most of what she is saying. I'm more and more unnerved. There's something quietly horrifying about not knowing who's speaking out from inside.

Helen: I suspect that she had a powerful flash of feeling at that moment that really moved her and probably shocked her, and that she felt good, filled with a sort of gladness and hope. But we don't know, and she's never said anything—not that we've heard her talk for more than twenty minutes—about any other experiences that would solidify into something that could support her in her life.

Chloe: Wait. She does have something else that gave her support and that was the true-crime circle, where she also felt a sense of community. It seems when she no longer felt seen by the Baptist family, she leant on this other group.

Sarah: As she sensed—or projected—the Pattersons withdrawing, which we know she resented, perhaps she migrated towards the people online.

Chloe: From *God is Love* she looked at what people do when full of hate.

In the time before her meeting Simon Patterson, Erin's life was complex. In June 2004, she pleaded guilty to five charges relating to a car crash in Glen Waverley. At almost three times the legal alcohol limit, she had been driving an unregistered car at 95 km/h in a 60 zone. She didn't stop after the crash. She was convicted, fined $1000 and her licence was cancelled for two and a half years.

Chloe: Whatever had happened in her young adulthood, as Helen's said, entering this family might have felt like the solution to shame.

Helen: Like cleaning up your act.

Sarah: I'm worthy of being loved. I'm worthy of being one of these people.

Chloe: A curtain will come down and there'll be a second act now. All that sin is in the past.

Sarah: But a true sentence hits the ear in a particular way. Eventually I started listening with the thought, If I had known her before all this happened, would I have trusted her? To the degree that I can answer that, I don't think I would. There's something there, and I don't know what it is. It could be extraordinary pain and trauma, or it could be mental disturbance, or it could be moral culpability—the evil that had a choice. But there's something there that doesn't hang together with the self that's being presented to the jury, and it's jarring.

Helen: I know people who, while they're talking, make me think, I don't believe a word of this. Not factually—something deeper is off. Everybody's got to create a persona, of course. No one can walk around in the world with their soul bared. It's got to be shielded and veiled in some way, just so you can stand the stress of being alive. But the false self is something more impermeable. A false self is like a glass that's pretending to be crystal. You tap it with a spoon, it rings dully or it doesn't ring. It looks good and you drink out of it and you could wash it but, somehow, when you hit it, it doesn't make a proper ring.

Sarah: I was thinking about how Ian and the family are in court each day—and how legal justice sits with divine justice. I was in Wonnangatta, up in the mountains, a few weeks ago, and there was a little cemetery that dates back to the 1860s. One headstone was for a three-year-old, and it just says, 'Thy Will Be Done'. And now I'm looking at Ian thinking, Do you consider yourself saved for a purpose? It would be hard in his shoes to think otherwise. And if you've devoted your life to that belief—thy will be done—what do you do with that?

Helen: You can't help feeling very warmly towards Ian Wilkinson and his family. A lot of this stuff has been news to them. It's horrible, and it gets more and more distressing as the weeks go on. They're sitting there, bearing witness to the working out of what happened to his wife and their mother, and trying to understand it. When I first heard the pastor giving evidence, I thought of that line from the Bible that Tolstoy uses as the epigraph to *Anna Karenina*: 'Vengeance is Mine, saith the Lord, I will repay.' I think it's saying, 'You don't have to take vengeance. I will deal with that. It'll all stack up in the end, and I'll see to it.' It's God speaking.

Chloe: Erin decided to do the vengeance part herself. But the people who'll feel her punishment most acutely are her kids. They're the people who…

Helen: …it will all land on in the long run. All along I've been thinking that she probably is guilty, not that she probably would be found guilty. Today was the first time I thought I wouldn't be surprised if this jury took mercy on her. I don't know if that feeling will last. But I felt for her today in a much deeper way than I had before. The gap between her and me shrank down really small.

I just came away distressed and bewildered, bewildered like I have been ever since I first heard this story.

Wednesday, 4 June 2025

TWO DAYS LATER Erin Patterson is still telling an elaborate tale: at the time of the lunch she had high hopes for the future. She was landscaping her garden and planned to study midwifery. She was booked in for a pre-surgical screening for gastric band surgery. She had indeed lied to Gail, Don, Heather and Ian about having cancer because she knew she would need to explain her sudden weight loss and felt too embarrassed to tell them her real plans. Erin says she has suffered low self-esteem all her life. When she was a child, she says, her mother constantly weighed her, and she had secretly been a long-term bulimic. Erin tearfully tells the court that, after the lunch guests left, she found the orange cake that Heather had brought. Two-thirds of it remained. She gorged slice after slice and then made herself vomit.

Helen is now back in Melbourne and, during the lunch break, the three of us walk along William Street outside the Supreme Court where we have been watching Erin on the screen.

Sarah: I don't believe it, but it does hang together as a story.

Helen: It hangs together brilliantly. It's seamless.

Chloe: It's starting to fray, though. She can be very precise but she grows vague around the lunch.

Sarah: Yeah, there are facts that are nipping at the edges. The jury has heard she served herself on a different-coloured plate.

Chloe: Her in-laws are in hospital, she knows they're gravely sick, and yet she gives her children the leftovers of the meal.

Sarah: Her four guests are in hospital, on fluids, after eating lunch at her house, yet, in her telling, they were just 'a bit unwell'. She never asked after them. And Mandy's not asking her anything about them. They don't figure at all. And then over everything else is the fact that she's a liar. We've heard her admit to lying about a million things, but now we're supposed to believe she's being honest about this one thing.

I'm exhausted by it—and then, with the cake—the opera! 'I had a slice of cake, and then another! And then another!' and her voice kept getting higher, like it was *Rigoletto*. Enough already with this. I don't have the emotion left. I'm exhausted, woman.

Chloe: What do you think, Helen? Do you believe her?

Helen: Well, I'm trying to listen to her like somebody who

doesn't know anything. I'm trying to scrub away all the stuff that I know, and I find her horribly believable. Even the stuff about the slices of cake.

If she actually did it, this is one of the most brilliant performances I've ever seen in my life. If she didn't do it, then it's fair dinkum. And I'm sitting there and I feel like she's forcing me to trust what she's saying. I look at her on the screen, and I can see her face so well. It's a face out of a myth. It's not like a modern person's face. It's a face of deep unhappiness, bone-deep wretchedness. But there's this mind in there, this mind.

Sarah: Her tone vacillates between feigning ignorance and being pointedly clever. Low energy and high energy. But, in a way, that's life. It's true she's a liar. But liars can still be not guilty of murder.

Chloe: We know that she's a good liar because the lunch ended with her guests all praying for her cancer.

Sarah: How many lies can the jury discount?

Chloe: And every time she now apologises for one, and says how ashamed and embarrassed she is, you feel she's actually apologising for the poisoning.

❖

Chloe: How about the fact Erin once opened a bookshop,

and that she travelled around collecting used books to stock in it?

Sarah: Yeah, back when they were living in Western Australia, Erin rented a space to open a bookshop.

Helen: That seems to me a grace note. I think it's unnecessary to mention it.

Chloe: Is this real? I thought, listening to her describe it. I dreamt about a bookshop, remember? She probably had some of your books, she might have had mine.

Helen: Chloe's first novel is called *A Child's Book of True Crime*—ha ha.

Chloe: Is there a link between Erin's mum's study of children's books and the bizarre tales Erin's telling now?

Sarah: I noticed how the choice of beef Wellington links to Erin's mum—it was a dish she made on special occasions.

Helen: They showed Erin's shopping list. Big share packs of lollies, chocolates and doughnuts. You've got to decide whether you believe the bulimia or not.

Sarah: She has lied about so many things. This is a person who has exploited any possible medical issue, including fictional ones. Vomiting for thirty years comes with significant gastrointestinal issues and dental issues, of which there's no evidence. And we're asked to believe she was silent about all of those forever?

In the police interview, Eppingstall says to her, You are here because your four lunch guests are very sick, and we're interested in why you are not. Remember that line? She needed to come up with an excuse that's fit for purpose. Here it is.

Chloe: We know she was given a computer in custody. I bet she's gone through every single piece of prosecution evidence and she's retrofitted this amazing story—including that she had thrown up the poison.

Sarah: We don't even know if vomiting would do any good.

Helen: What about the new story to account for her 'acute diarrhoea'—how does it go?

Sarah: The day after the lunch, she drove her son to the flying lesson. And it was a two-hour round trip on which she only went to the toilet at the petrol station. But now she claims she also pulled over, with both kids in the car, to a stretch of bushland outside Nyora. She goes into the bush, has diarrhoea, cleans herself up with tissues, puts the tissues in a dog poo bag, puts that in her handbag, and takes it back to the car. Then, in the petrol station toilet, she drops the poo bag in the bin, and buys some sandwiches for her children. I don't think any of that is true, except for the sandwiches.

Helen: Why didn't she just put a leaf over it?

Sarah: The whole thing's implausible.

Chloe: There's been way too much talk about poo in this trial.

Simon Patterson had testified that the day after the lunch Erin claimed she feared she would 'poo her pants' and, while ferrying the children to their activities, remained seated in the car in the hope this would function as 'a cork'. Erin had presented hospital staff with a faecal sample, saying that her 'poo looked like a wee'. She was conscious of the consistency of her diarrhoea because, 'as a mum', she was well acquainted with the Bristol Stool Scale, a diagnostic tool used to classify faecal matter. The doctors, nurses and barristers had spoken at length about their and others' observations of Erin's bowel movements. Her molecular faecal test detected no *Amanita phalloides* pathogens.

Chloe: Way too much scatological business.

Helen: What if you're just an ordinary person, like me, who is really interested in shit?

Sarah: Me too.

Chloe: I feel judged. This is wild. She is wild.

Helen: My sanity point in all this wildness is Detective Eppingstall from the Homicide Squad.

Sarah: His skull is boulder-shaped, and he himself is a rock.

Chloe: But, in the witness box, Erin's at sea and then suddenly she changes. She had to wait alone during a short break in proceedings and you could see that fast mind thinking, What have I said? What do I need to say next? Her eyes were moving quickly from side to side as if scanning a script.

Helen: The awful thing about all her lies is you don't know how deep they go and how far back they go.

Chloe: I think they go far back…

Helen: …to adolescence?

Sarah: She lies to herself, which is why she can lie with such conviction. Or she believes that, regardless of the truth, she's entitled to be believed. She fully inhabits the lies.

Chloe: It's so Munchausen, though. She admitted she went on with her lies about cancer because she loved the attention Gail was giving her.

Sarah: I wrote it down. Hold on—this was the lie about having an elbow tumour. 'I didn't want their care of me to stop. I shouldn't have done it.' *It* applies to the lunch.

❖

In court, Erin lists a variety of suspected ailments requiring procedures for both her and her children. If a doctor wouldn't agree to a procedure, it seemed she found another doctor.

Mandy questions her, in particular, about her ongoing concern about ovarian cancer. In 2021, she'd suffered a multitude of symptoms.

> I felt very fatigued. I had ongoing abdominal pain. I had chronic headaches. I put on a lot of weight in quite a short period of time—my feet and my hands seemed to retain a lot of fluid. And what set me over the edge to actually go to the doctor was my wedding rings suddenly wouldn't fit, and so I took them to the local jeweller to be resized. And only a few weeks later when I picked them up, they—like, my hands had outgrown them again.

Chloe: This sounds like perimenopause—but it's also like a fairytale. A wedding ring knows the truth about its wearer. Every time she tells a lie, the ring shrinks. She grows bigger. The ring gets smaller and smaller.

Mandy asked about an MRI referral.
'On my head, is that the one you are referring to, my brain?'
'Yes. And why did that happen?'
'I'd been suffering chronic headaches that were getting more intense and more frequent and, once again, I turned to Dr Google and convinced myself I had a brain tumour or a brain disease.'
'The notes say, "Erin is wondering if we should organise spinal MRI, as her brain MRI is normal."'

'That's correct.'

'So you had a brain MRI?'

'I did.'

'And then you wanted—?'

'I wanted more: a rheumatologist, a general physician, a cardiologist.'

'So your concerns had moved from ovarian cancer to brain lymphoma and then on to heart conditions and MS?'

'That's right, yep.'

Chloe: There's also Munchausen-by-proxy to consider. Do you think she wanted to just make them very sick and then rush around and look after them?

Sarah: Okay, so at the start of today, Erin said she invited them over because she could sense there was a growing distance. 'I needed to be proactive' is how she put it. She had the panic of being left behind, being cut out. We can assume she was in an inflamed, agitated state—this is the month where she's pulled the kids out of school...

Helen: ...without asking Simon first.

Sarah: So you sense the growing distance—that's the reason for bringing everyone together for a loving lunch. But it would be the same motive for killing them, eliminating the source of the panic-inducing feelings.

Chloe: I understand why she might have wanted to kill

Simon. But why did she decide that she was going to take them all out?

Sarah: Remember how she told her barrister why she initially refused to stay at the hospital? She said, 'I couldn't move my brain.' She was stuck in her plan for the day. She said, 'It was like trying to turn a really, really big ship, it takes a long time.' It was her plan, until the very last moment, for Simon not to survive this lunch. Perhaps she sensed he and the family were closing ranks.

Thursday, 5 June 2025

WE ARE BALLOTED A media pass in the Morwell courtroom. Sarah drives to the Latrobe Valley, and Helen and Chloe watch in the media room at the Supreme Court. During the lunch break the three of us have a phone call.

Chloe: We're squatting in an office on the twenty-fourth floor of Owen Dixon Chambers. You should see the gallery of portraits we had to wade through to find the lift—all these gentlemen barristers and judges, one after the other.

Helen: Okay, this is day twenty-seven of the trial. There has been a tremendous change of gear this morning, and it's made us sit up. We've just come from watching the prosecutor's first chance to cross-examine Erin.

Mandy's been taking it very slowly and carefully, inching along. And then, suddenly, Nanette Rogers—

Chloe: —did a bull out of the gate.

Helen: She came blazing through.

Chloe: It was exciting to feel this different pace, the shock and awe. But the judge gave Rogers a note that she might be too fast for the jury...

Helen: ...and he asked her to break her sentences down.

Chloe: There's so much evidence, which the jurors navigate on iPads. She needed to give them time to toggle between files.

Sarah: Is it what you expected?

Helen: I don't even know what I'm expecting anymore. I'm finding this whole experience so bizarre. Nothing that's happening is familiar to me, tonally or psychologically, and I think that's why I keep going to sleep. I've fallen several times into really deep sleep, not just that nervous nodding off that you do if you're bored. I'm not bored. I feel that I'm trying to defend myself against something by going to sleep.

Erin Patterson sits there, her face like a tragic mask from some ancient civilisation. She sits very still, but I can see her hands under the table she's sitting at, and they're constantly moving.

Chloe: She's twisting her glasses...

Sarah: ...and a tissue. She's moulding it, moulding it, moulding it. Her hands are always moving under that desk.

Chloe: We've seen photos in the paper of crowds outside the Morwell court. And one journalist told us that people in the courtroom are taking selfies with Erin behind them.

What's the atmosphere like, Sarah?

Sarah: It's super crowded, and small subgroups have formed: court friends who came together and people who came individually and now sit together. There's a gleefulness that I find repellent—laughing and looking over at her. One pair of women took photos in the courtroom. If the tipstaff had seen that, it wouldn't have been tolerated.

But we have to look at our own interest in the case. Is it any different from that gleeful, ogling schadenfreude? Or from those people who are giving her greasies and making sure she sees their dirty looks? I don't think it's self-exonerating to say it's different, and I'm not saying we're here as lofty, self-appointed guardians of the social fabric, but there's no glee for me in being here.

Chloe: Helen talked about falling asleep as a defence. I think that kind of glee could also be a type of defence: This wouldn't happen to my family, this wouldn't happen to me, I am not like this.

Sarah: It allows you to feel better about all the times in your own life when you let rage or resentment take the wheel. But the falling asleep, yeah, I feel that exhaustion. A plug has been pulled out, and my energy just drains. I can barely open my eyes in the room. And it was the same yesterday. It's been the same since Erin took the stand.

There's a pattern in her answers, over these last days, of feigned civility while she's as obstructive and oppositional as possible. There's also feigned ignorance—I don't know where I bought the mushrooms. I don't know which grocery shop. I don't know whether I went to Loch when the phone pings there. I don't know if I foraged for mushrooms that day. I don't know if that's my kitchen bench. I don't know if I took that photo. She's a stranger, even to herself, is the picture we're getting. And, as I read in a review by Alison Croggon the other day, 'estrangement from the self is the heart of horror'.

Helen: Erin seems to have decided which lies she's going to frankly admit that she's told. That is a very interesting manoeuvre. I'm not sure if she's going to be able to keep a handle on it. When Mandy said to her this morning, 'Tell me, why did you tell the police these lies about the dehydrator?' And she said, 'It was just a stupid kneejerk reaction to dig deeper and keep lying.' I was struck by that. I don't know if she meant dig myself deeper into the shit. It's as if to dig deeper, for her, means that she gets down to where everything is false.

Chloe: At the end of Mandy's examination, he asked her whether or not she'd deliberately done harm to the relatives. She was distraught and crying and, in this dramatic and painful moment, she reached for a tissue. But when the cross-examination started and Nanette Rogers came at her with ferocity, Erin's affect instantly changed. The tissue in her hand was no longer needed. She became belligerent, with her smartest-person-in-the-room tone, and I don't think the jury would have liked it.

Helen: I saw that as a big shot of adrenaline that went through her. When Mandy was in charge, she sat there like a pudding. Now she's energised. If somebody like Nanette Rogers came at you the way she's coming at Erin now, you'd sit bolt upright. You'd think, Right, it's on. But as soon as she started to get bolshy, I felt myself bristling. When she was asked why she was putting mushrooms in her children's food, she said sarcastically, 'I was trying to add more veggies into my children's bodies.'

Chloe: I couldn't help thinking, You *were* trying to add things to other bodies.

Sarah: I love watching Nanette in action. For all our talk about the taboo against female aggression, her manner is appropriate to the circumstances. It's required. It's necessary. Everything she's saying is relevant. In other trials I've seen cross-examination so aggressive that it makes you want to flee from the room. It's almost intolerable. But she has such a dignified way of going about it. There's a line of homicide detectives sitting directly behind her, and they all have looks of vindication on their faces.

It's also a joy watching Beale think when he hears submissions from counsel in the absence of the jury. The animated eyebrows, the slow gait of his sentences as he works through each side's argument, how his palms face each other and move together to the left and right as his logic path moves. He thinks in conversation but concludes alone. I like how plainly he says, 'I am against you, Mr Mandy.'

Helen: Rogers is taking that old-style teacher's tone. She's pushing really hard, in a way that suggests Erin Patterson actually owes her answers.

Wednesday, 9 June 2025

Chloe: Erin has now disagreed with every single witness. She's disagreed with Simon. She's disagreed with Ian, with what Heather said about the orange plate. She's disagreed with her brother-in-law's and her sister-in-law's recollections, with the child protection officer, the informant, and the doctors and nurses.

Sarah: No one else is correct about anything. Or she's forgotten.

Chloe: She can't bear any story involving her if she's not the storyteller.

Helen: I don't blame her. I'd probably be the same. She splits hairs about the meanings of words…

Chloe: …with a hard kind of quickness.

Sarah: She pretends confusion, then makes her little semantic critiques: 'Sorry, I was confused by the double negatives.'

Helen: Or she talks back! She said to Nanette, 'You're going to have to rephrase that, so I know what you're talking about.'

Sarah: It was like watching a jellyfish tentacle move under the water to give a little sting and then sneak out of sight.

Tuesday, 10 June 2025

WE ARE BALLOTED ANOTHER media ticket to be in court for Erin's seventh day on the stand. This time Chloe drives to Morwell and takes it. Sarah and Helen watch from the Supreme Court in Melbourne.

Chloe: There was a shimmer of exhaustion in the court. Erin was the only person who got up with gusto for the judge. She was wearing a paisley shirt, black pants and open-toed sandals. Her skin was now a grey colour under heavy makeup, thick bronze or gold eye shadow, and she was blinking almost non-stop. She walked past me to the witness stand, carrying some papers. Nanette wanted to know what they were and the judge asked her. Erin said they were photos of her children. He told her to pass them to her solicitor.

   Nanette went straight on the attack: the Enrich Clinic, where she said Erin claimed to have booked in for gastric band surgery, turns out to be a dermatological salon that doesn't do surgical procedures.

Erin said, 'Oh!' and went blank.

Nanette asked her about her death cap research. Erin didn't remember ever visiting iNaturalist. She said, 'Somebody did and that somebody could have been me.'

Nanette kept shifting the ground. She went to Erin's arrival at Leongatha Hospital. She said the doctor recognised her.

Sarah: His reaction to her must have given something away. It was obvious she was surprised the medicos had worked out pretty fast what the poison was.

Chloe: She told the court she was completely shocked to hear about death caps. Then she started talking about her diarrhoea.

> Rogers: I suggest you were not seriously unwell because you did not consume even a minute amount of death cap mushrooms at the lunch. What do you say?
>
> Patterson: I have no idea if I did or I didn't.
>
> Rogers: You were not suffering from death cap mushroom poisoning.
>
> Patterson: Incorrect.
>
> Rogers: You deliberately tried to make it look like you were.
>
> Patterson: Incorrect.
>
> Rogers: You did that because you knew you had not eaten death cap mushrooms and you knew how suspicious it

would look if you did not seem sick like your guests.

Patterson: Incorrect.

Chloe: The consistency of Erin's diarrhoea was brought up. She was quite haughty about being au fait with the Bristol Stool Chart. She actually said to Nanette Rogers, 'Don't know if you have any experience of it?'

The fatigue in the courtroom is off the chart.

As Erin kept going, I wanted to yell out.

Sarah: Yell what?

Chloe: *Stop!*

The women watching her in the public seats were all sitting forward, listening intently. Notebooks open, pens in hand. I kept thinking they could be Erin. In Erin's old life, she would have been one of the women watching the trial. I could picture her, getting up early, driving here and spending her day absorbed in someone else's marital disaster. Everyone in this court is probably somewhere on the domestic spectrum from moderately to desperately disappointed.

When the court adjourned for lunch, Erin stood and walked back to the dock. She saw her power of attorney—and the power of attorney is herself a great character: long straight hair, wearing a chic poncho and carrying under her arm the latest Liane Moriarty mystery, *Here One Moment*.

A warm smile came over Erin's face. She gave the power of attorney a look of relief: *finally a break*, but at the edges of her mouth were complicated feelings. There was this twist in the smile. For a millisecond, behind the mask, you could see a glint of dark humour—what's underneath her blankness is not straightforward.

Helen, here's a brain-twister for you. The mobile-phone evidence shows that when Erin left the hospital for the first time—after they told her she needed life-saving medication—she drove to Outtrim, which is where the mycologist had seen *Amanita phalloides* growing. Why did she go back there?

Sarah: Chloe has had an intuitive understanding of why, which has made me now terrified to be alone with her.

Chloe: Did she go there to eat a tiny bit of death cap mushroom…

Sarah: …because she wasn't sick enough?

Chloe: She knows that she hasn't ingested the same meal as her guests and won't have the same symptoms. I just can't see any other reason she'd have driven back there.

Helen: Maybe she was worried that she'd left something behind? You know, a 'clue'?

Chloe: I don't think the death caps are going to have, like, fingerprints on them!

Sarah: I do think she would have gone to get a tiny bit to make herself sicker. Then obviously she thought again.

Helen: She knows from her research how much the lethal dose was. This is giving me the willies.

Sarah: In the closing addresses, we'll get each side of the story. At this stage, even Justice Beale doesn't know with certainty what picture the defence is about to put together. We've been getting the pieces, and it's only now, in week eight, that we learn what we were looking at this whole time. It's a wild way of telling a story. Plus, every extra day increases the risk of something fucking up with the jury. They are really are up against it.

Helen: Before I forget, can I read you this bit from my diary: 'Last night I had a weird dream. I was on my knees, digging in some damp, dark soil. I saw a chubby whitish-grey object and I pulled it out. It was a mushroom. The more I dug, the more of them I found. They smelt delicious and murky. But I knew they were very dangerous and I must resist the temptation to eat them on the spot.'

❖

The next day Chloe drives Helen home to Melbourne.

Helen: I feel like I lose all my friends for the duration of a trial. They ring up and say, 'Do you want to do this or that?'

and I can't. And I can't go out at night because I'm so tired. All the things that give shape and meaning to your life are overridden by the structure that a trial imposes. You can't predict how it's going to be until you're in the middle of it. And the only way to get out is to write or—in this case—to talk about it.

Chloe: Our friendship—yours and mine and Sarah's—has only deepened, though. I can see that Erin probably did feel a kinship with her Facebook true-crime friends. She probably did feel understood. We've been held together, too, in a tight bond.

Helen: Usually writing means you're thinking about it on your own all the time. It's a relief to be with someone who's familiar with the story and the people in it. You can just mention something and they know. But people say, 'So, how's it going?' I have this feeling that I can't possibly give a sensible account of the trial to someone who wasn't there. It's like being in a plane crash and the person sitting next to you also survived, and she was a stranger, but now you're linked forever.

Friday, 13 June 2025

After eight days in the witness box, Erin returns to the dock. We try to work out when next to drive to Morwell.

Helen: Hang on while I get my diary…Hang on a second…

Chloe: Guys, remember I'm going overseas on Wednesday. I'm sorry. I thought this was going to be over by now. While I'm away, I'll look after the transcripts. But you should make a time and record yourselves each day…Yeah, do record yourselves.

There are no recordings from 15 June to 30 June. Sarah and Helen, ill with COVID and flu respectively, listen from home.

Nanette Rogers spent two days delivering the Crown's closing arguments. 'The pieces of evidence are like pieces of a jigsaw puzzle,' she told the jury. 'One piece on its own might tell you not very much at all about what the picture is, but as you start putting more and more pieces together, and looking at it as a whole, the picture starts to become clear.

'The sinister deception was to use a nourishing meal as the vehicle to deliver the deadly poison.'

Colin Mandy delivered the defence's closing arguments across three days. 'If you think that it's *possible* that Erin deliberately poisoned the meal, you must find her not guilty,' he said. 'If you think that *maybe* Erin deliberately poisoned the meal you must find her not guilty. If you think that she *probably* deliberately poisoned the meal, you must find her not guilty.'

Justice Beale then read his 365-page charge to the jury, summarising the evidence of more than fifty witnesses and the law that applied to it. He concluded his charge on the fortieth day of the trial. 'When putting all the pieces together you must be careful not to jump to conclusions,' he told the jury. 'Don't let sympathy or prejudice cloud your judgment.' Their decision boiled down to one question: was it beyond reasonable doubt that Erin Patterson had deliberately used death cap mushrooms with the intention of killing her lunch guests or causing them serious injury?

PART VI

The Verdict

Monday, 30 June 2025

THE JURY GOES OUT to begin its deliberations.
From London, Chloe calls Sarah and Helen, who are driving home to Melbourne after their first day back at the courthouse.

Chloe: Tell me everything.

Sarah: We're into the next phase now. There was no verdict, they've only been deliberating for three hours. But there's a different vibe, for sure.

Chloe: What's the general feeling on which way it's going to go?

Sarah: Is there a general feeling?

Helen: Nobody's really saying. Since the jury's gone out, everyone's just been wandering around the town all day. We were standing in an op shop and the whole defence team came in.

Chloe: Tell me what the defence were thrifting for? Did Mandy buy anything?

Sarah: We brazenly asked—Mandy was looking for some Dr Seuss books for his kid. We were over near the books.

Helen: We had a quiet, pleasant conversation.

Sarah: The jury are sequestered. If there's no verdict by Friday, they've got to sit on Saturday. They won't sit on Sunday, but they can't go home. So I think there's a lot to be said for a Friday verdict—they will have put in about a week of effort to reach a verdict by that point.

Chloe: I'll get in the car on Friday.

Friday, 4 July 2025

Sarah drives Helen and Chloe back to Morwell. We have now heard that a number of Erin's Facebook acquaintances are writing or are contemplating writing books on the case. Erin's messages provide these authors with rich material. Erin has described the local Korumburra community as 'illiterate mother**kers'; she's posted about her cat suffering from mushroom poisoning, despite not owning a cat; and has written messages about her mother's death that have struck an odd tone. Erin shared photographs of books from her mother's curated library, thrown, with spines bent and crushed, into the back of her car. Erin had visited her mother in the month before her death.

Helen: In the beginning we felt womanly sympathy for her and then it started to fade. All thoughts of Erin's innocence have now been obliterated.

Sarah: Her personality seems slightly clearer at least. I'm

reading a book by Erich Fromm on human destructiveness. He talks about Freud's later work being less concerned with the basic sexual drives and more concerned with 'human passions'. Rather than just the fundamental drives of feeding and fucking or whatever—you also need meaning. The most life-embracing and highest expression of meaning being love and generosity. But in the absence of that capacity, Fromm says, the passions turn necrophilic—into a fascination with darkness, control and mechanisation.

Chloe: In other words—

Sarah: —a Facebook true-crime chat group, that's right. Or being on her various devices passionately researching death cap mushrooms…

And, it would later emerge, many other poisons.

Erin Patterson had accessed *Criminal Poisonings* (2007) on her Samsung tablet, saving one of its appendices—'Common Homicidal Poisons'.

She searched for 'hemlock', accessing a September 2022 iNaturalist post locating a suspected sighting of the poisonous plant at Loch in Gippsland.

She downloaded an article on barium carbonate—rat poison—around the time of Simon's third hospital admission.

She also downloaded fifty cases of red-kidney-bean poisoning in the UK from 1976 to 1989, a paper about extracting toxins from seeds titled 'One-step Purification and Characterisation of Abrin Toxin from Abrus Precatorius Seeds' and a 2011 journal, *Victorian Naturalist*, that referred to death cap mushrooms growing under oaks.

Amongst the cache found on her computer was also the *Scandinavian Journal of Trauma and Resuscitation Emergency Medicine*, which referred to medical error in treatment of *Amanita phalloides* poisoning in pre-hospital care.

Sarah: Her online life became a synthetic substitute for meaning and purpose and autonomy. But at the heart of that is fear and a very small person who is very helpless. There's the mind that won't turn off at night, and no real friends and no real marriage, many homes, and therefore no home.

Chloe: With a library with no books in it.

During cross-examination, when Nanette Rogers put it to Erin Patterson that the detectives had catalogued 423 books owned by her, none of which related to her stated passion for mushrooms or foraging, Erin said she had many more boxes of books in the garage still needing to be unpacked.

Chloe: I wonder if the boxes contained her mother's books?

Sarah: We won't know.

Chloe: Or were they the books from her bookshop, the failed

bookshop? I've found a Reddit thread speculating on books Erin may have read. Agatha Christie has a book with a poisoned mushroom stew. Someone has also posted: 'I bet she has this on the shelf' about Donna Tartt's mega-hit *The Secret History*. Apparently, in the novel, a group of students try to determine what dosage of death caps will kill their target while leaving them ill enough to avoid suspicion and liver damage. They plan to hide it in a meal.

Sarah: Oh, no.

Helen: If only *she'd* spent all that time writing stuff. Erin obviously enjoyed the act of writing. Those messages she sent to her parents-in-law, they're very, very skilfully and courteously composed. They've got perfect pacing and a striking command of tone.

Sarah: There's a photo in the *Age* of Erin's house. Someone's put privacy shields, big black tarps, around the exterior. Maybe it's in anticipation of Erin returning home.

Erin's power of attorney and Facebook friend is still in residence at the property.

Chloe: Imagine that you've joined this true-crime group and you've bonded with Erin and been drawn into this crime. And you *don't* think to yourself, Fuck this is weird, as weird as could be, I'm gonna write a book and make some cash.

Instead, you think, I'm going to defend this person to the hilt, and live in her empty house, and eat at the table where she poisoned her family.

Sarah: The power of attorney is now hanging out around the court with Simon's media adviser. They had lunch at the same table, but, also, the media adviser is chatty with the Real Housewives of Morwell. Everywhere I look the root systems are intertwining. It's like we're about to graduate together.

Out the car window the view becomes dimmer.

Chloe: Oh, no, it's the Mushroom Trial Fog.

Sarah: This is a fog that kicks in right before Moe.

Chloe: God, there's a lot of fog.

Sarah: Actually, this is the clearest it's been.

Helen: Some days you could only dimly see the trees.

Sarah: We'll spend the day perched on the seats outside Courtroom Four. The bathrooms are right there. We can go for lunch, but we have to be back by 2.15 because the verdict's most likely to come in the afternoon. Do you think it will be today, or is that just wishful thinking?

Helen: Both. Maybe.

Chloe: If it doesn't happen today, I'll be a bit nervous that it'll be a hung jury.

Sarah: I know, we'll worry about that later.

Helen: Today feels like a stop for me. I don't know where we can go with this. Oh, this is real fog.

Chloe: I do feel like somehow Erin has cast it.

Sarah: I had that thought as well, like somehow she's conjured from the subterranean cell, from her furrowed brow, this haze which has sprung forth fully formed.

Chloe: It's a miasma of *why?*

Helen: I actually feel quite scared of her.

Sarah: It is frightening. She was so calculating to do this in such a horrific way and ruin the lives of her children, but there's the slight little seam of absurdity that if she was actually as smart as she thought, she wouldn't have found herself in this courtroom having her faeces dissected for ten weeks.

Helen: I think she knows how to read our notebooks through our bags.

   Something just struck me. Her mother had the same name as one of the dead women.

Sarah: There are two Heathers. And Erin served the women her own mother's special dish.

As we reach Morwell, Sarah has to turn on the headlights. The thick fog has a sepia tone due to the brown dust coming off the open-cut coalmine.

It has grown colder and wetter over the last ten weeks. Mushrooms are growing in the garden beds of the motels near the courthouse.

Outside Courtroom Four, the clock is stuck on five to eleven.

Helen: I'm worried about that clock. I want to fix it. It shouldn't be stuck on that time. It's been stuck there for two days. Maybe I should tell that nice security guard. If he would get it down, I could put in a new battery. At my own expense.

We sit down and wait.

A man in his seventies who's been observing the trial comes and sits opposite.

Helen: Everything's gone flat.

Man: We need closure. We need to be able to get on with our lives.

He says he has bought a rosewood mahogany coffin and a headstone of black marble for $6500.

Helen: I want a wicker basket.

He says the lid of his friend's coffin wasn't screwed down properly and the friend fell out and went rolling down the hill and it took six people to get him back in. He thinks maybe the man's grandson playing the violin had triggered something.

Helen goes to talk to Kelly, the dairy farmer.

Chloe: I can't handle this. Maybe it's jetlag.

Behind us, one woman says to another, 'It's worth waiting around for the verdict. You can say you were a part of history.'

Helen returns.

Helen: Kelly just got a tiny red mushroom tattoo on her forearm. She showed it to me. The colour has fallen out a bit because there was a scab, so she's going back for a free touch-up.

During the lunch break we walk to the cafe where the defence, the Crown, the Homicide Squad, the journalists and the trial spectators also often go for lunch.

Sarah: Any particular weirdness in having been away and coming back to this, Chloe?

Chloe: All of the same characters are here but in configurations that should only happen in a dream.

One of the court security guards asks Helen and Sarah for publishing advice. Outside the court, the reporter in the powder-blue coat is brushing her hair and talking to the trial spectators. Erin Patterson's power of attorney approaches us with a packet of Uno cards and invites us to play a game with her.

Sarah: Boundaries collapsing.

Chloe: This is how it feels on mushrooms—all your edges blur.

Helen: Rainbow Man was probably tripping the whole time.

Sarah: That's the other thing about covering a trial—it becomes a community. There was a sociologist called Victor Turner who wrote about something called 'communitas': how strangers who go through a big experience together form an intense bond. The usual social order dissolves. This is one of those times. I can feel it, the energy of it—it's like a contagion.

Chloe: Like a fever dream, everybody's sort of…

Helen: …bouncing it off each other.

Sarah: It's not like a moral panic, but it has the same sort of infectious energy.

Chloe: And yet, even in this lunchroom, it's like nothing's changed.

Helen: I asked the journalist in the powder-blue coat about her motel. And she said, 'It's really nice, but next door there's this halfway house, and every night there are screams and fights and people cursing. A woman tried to throw a brick through my window.'

Sarah: The journos make a family. The jury is its own family. Court staff is its own family. The lawyers, the rusted-on members of the public. Maybe you earn your place in the group, like you do in any group, by virtue of sheer endurance.

Chloe: There's this strange party atmosphere.

Sarah: We've all gone through something together. It's ten weeks now. We've seen these people probably more than we've seen our own families.

Helen: Here comes Mandy. Don't make eye contact.

The jury does not return. It quickly grows dark on the drive back to Melbourne.

Helen: Well, that was pretty demoralising. I'm sure waiting's really bad for people. There was a light hysteria hanging over the court. Everyone was on a hair trigger but pretending to be cool. What about that group photo?

Chloe: Yeah, I saw it.

Helen: Those seats outside Courtroom Four have a view right onto the concrete courtyard. And suddenly there was a pandemonium out on the street where the TV vans are parked, and scores of journos and camera crews came pouring down the side of the building and milled around madly in the yard. There must have been fifty of them, or more. Then somebody ran out with a ladder and stood it in front of the bloc, and Kelly in her overalls climbed up the ladder and stood near the top. She had a camera. Everyone stood still and looked up at her, she aimed the camera and the whole lot of them threw their arms in the air and gave a huge cheer, like a footy team that's just won a flag.

Chloe: It must have been partly the pent-up—

Helen: Yeah, everyone's sort of finished.

Sarah: But this is a murder trial. The centre has to hold, most of all now.

Chloe recounts having spoken at lunch to a community lawyer who grew up in the region. He suggested Erin Patterson might have chosen to hold her trial in Morwell because there was a greater chance in this jurisdiction for a mistrial. Each extra day of deliberation seems to raise this as a possibility.

Helen: I think if it's a hung jury, we put it down and walk away.

Chloe: What? And we don't do anything with the tapes?

Helen: We don't do anything. You'd have to do it without me. I'm not doing it.

Sarah: I would be characterologically incapable of not going to a retrial.

Helen: I don't think I would feel like that. I feel that I would be glad to escape from it.

Sarah: There is no escaping from it now that I'm in it. It's like quicksand.

Helen: I know it's mean and it's ignorant, but I'm mad at the jury today. I haven't felt mad at them before. Come on, take a fucking risk, do something.

Sarah: I've thought of them unkindly since Wednesday afternoon.

Helen: I don't really believe in the devil, but I do believe that people become possessed by evil. You can talk about it in a psychological way—that she's very, very twisted. But there's this great wretched darkness that she seems to reveal. I have a horrible sense of her as a kind of black hole, a vortex.

Chloe: We're in the vortex. We've been in it for ten weeks.

Sarah: We should feel nervous—we're finding out how

much we'll never know.

Chloe: My mind has hit a wall.

Sarah: It needs to end.

Helen: I panicked in the car driving here. I thought I would like to get out of this. I would like to run. And then I thought, Wait a minute.

Chloe: Sarah's locked the car doors.

Sarah: That's why I have child locks.

Helen: I thought we're too far in to go back, and the only way out is straight ahead and through.

Sarah: I'm aware this is going to sound deranged, but I feel you can get caught in the darkness and attract more darkness.

Helen: What I don't want is to write something that's going to attract her animus.

Chloe: You don't want a hex?

Helen: A hex, or even just her attention. I don't want her looking at me. I want to be the one doing the looking.

I found some stuff in an old notebook the other day about a Brothers Grimm tale called 'The Little Shroud'. A woman's young son dies, and she's grief-stricken. She cries all the time, she keeps his things by her, and is destroyed by his death. One night he appears to her in his shroud. He begs her to stop grieving for him, because her tears are soaking the shroud and stopping him from falling asleep—and from being free, keeping him from the freedom of being dead.

Chloe: The Pattersons must be unable to grieve properly or get on with their lives.

Helen: And that's another awful thing about it dragging on like this. Nobody talks or thinks about those dear people. And when Justice Beale spoke after the jury directions, when he said, 'We have to remember that three people have died,' I thought he was saying in a coded way, Why doesn't everyone stop emoting and rushing around and drawing attention to themselves? There's got to be a moment of realisation of what this is actually about.

The three of us have now recorded hours of our conversations and we have to make up our minds what we have been doing here. A podcast we'd started making has fallen over and sometimes the book we are still loosely imagining feels as if it might do the same.

Chloe: It was an act of trust to take on this project together. I looked back at some notes and was surprised to see that we've been doing this since May. Time has concertinaed: the trial feels like it's another world that we only entered for a moment. But we were there for months.

Helen: It's true, but that's connected to the travelling we had to do.

Chloe: I think it was the company, though, too. It was each other's company.

Helen: If you go to some phenomenon by yourself, you are where the buck stops. You can get lost and panic. But when I'm with you two, because I trust both of you, and I trust your aesthetic, or goal, I can relax. There are three minds working on this, and when we're rolling along, and we're talking, I get a feeling of great rightness: that I'm thinking and feeling at the same time. If there's three streams of that flowing at once, I know that I don't have to worry that I'm out on a limb.

O N SATURDAY, 5 JULY, Sarah drives to Morwell on her own. There is no verdict. She drives home.

On Sunday, 6 July, the jury, sequestered in a local hotel, do not deliberate.

On Monday, 7 July, Sarah again drives to Morwell alone. During the lunch hour, an email notifies the media that the jury has reached its decision. Sarah is in the courtroom for the verdict. Afterwards she calls Helen and Chloe from the car.

Sarah: I'm just leaving Morwell. The sun's going down.

Chloe: Are you okay, Kras, to drive?

Sarah: I'm still sweating. I'm so bedraggled. I was in the loo at the cafe, I came back to my table and took a sip of my coffee, which had just arrived. And you rang and said, 'Did you get the email?' And I was like, 'What?' because I'd been refreshing my email all morning, and I was watching the defence team who were in the corner, eating lunch. And

I was like, 'What email?' And then everybody in the cafe suddenly shot up and there was a scrum round the cash register and the staff were like, 'No—go. Pay later.' And then we were all running, like really running to the court. There was no dignity.

I got in and I sat in the seat directly in front of Erin, in that back pew. She was impassive. I could hear her breathing. It was *sigh-gasp-sigh*. The room quietened down as soon as Justice Beale and the jury came in.

Helen: Tell us what the jury looked like?

Sarah: When they filed in, I got a little nervous. I've always thought that if they don't look at the person it means they're about to deliver a guilty verdict. But three of them looked at her.

Helen: Were they men or women who looked at her?

Sarah: They were men. But it was quick. Here we go, I thought. The judge's associate stood and asked the foreperson for the first verdict: 'How say you on charge one of the attempted murder of Ian Wilkinson, do you find Erin Patterson guilty or not guilty?'

'Guilty.'

He named and numbered each charge and each victim.

For the murder of Heather Wilkinson?

'Guilty.'

For the murder of Gail Patterson?

'Guilty.'

For the murder of Don Patterson?

'Guilty.'

I looked at Erin right after that first 'guilty', and there was no expression on her face beyond mild interest.

Normally, when I'm in the room for the verdict, there's this energy, my heart races, my hands shake. Today it was not there. It was not there because the family weren't there. It was strangely anticlimactic. Justice Beale put a date in the diary for the sentencing hearing. Then he thanked the jury for their service and praised them for their diligence. They filed out. Everyone was told to leave the court so Colin Mandy could have some time with Erin.

On my way out, I looked through the glass panel of the door to one of those little meeting rooms. I saw the female homicide detective reach up and give Eppingstall such a hug. It was a very human little moment to glimpse. Then I saw Simon's media adviser give Eppingstall a huge hug, then, when I turned around, the power of attorney was weeping and hugging the media adviser.

Chloe: Tell us about the scrum afterwards. Helen and I saw it on the TV news. What was it like to be there?

Sarah: Very deranged. Everyone was outside waiting. I looked from that high window down into the courtyard, and it was just this wave, this wall of cameras advancing towards the building. The power of attorney came out the door, and they formed a tight little pack around her and jostled her down the stairs. Then it happened again with Mandy and the defence team. It was quite physical. Cameramen were knocking into each other.

Chloe: It sounds as though Erin didn't really react either, at the end.

Sarah: They must have taken her out of the court through the tunnel that leads to the police station. But before they took her out? No, no expression. No. *You want an expression from me? Fuck you. You're not getting an expression.*

Chloe: The ancient mask.

Sarah: They've just released photos taken earlier in the trial—the ones I texted you guys of Erin in the prison van.

Helen: I was shocked by the first photo they screened on TV, the one taken through the window of the van. It made her look so ugly. I was angry. I thought, Now they're going to kill her in every way. I felt sick, really. How can you do this? You know her life is over.

Sarah: There was that witch-trial aspect. Okay, Erin is guilty. She murdered three people. But you know how they feast on a woman? Photographers are big-game hunters, and those are the prize shots. I saw one of them showing the security guards his series of photos: 'Yeah, we got into the van, look at this!' It was like a carnival. There was something dehumanising in that glee.

Chloe: It's interesting though, isn't it, the idea that the rent in the social fabric gets healed when she's driven off in the van.

Sarah: Yeah, what has been hidden is now manifest.

Chloe: Or it's taken from sight. It's put in the van so you don't have to see it.

Sarah: And now everyone can feel purged.

Helen: Have they taken her to Dame Phyllis Frost prison?

Sarah: Yes, I believe so.

Chloe: The shots of her face contorting in the van remind me of those old Charcot photos…

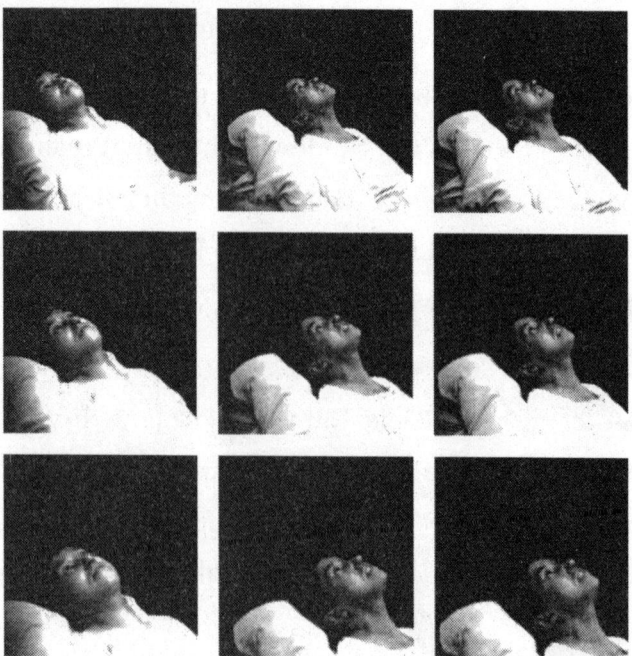

Helen: Oh, my Lord—women in asylums in the time of Freud.

Sarah: Were they driven crazy? Did life drive Erin crazy, or was her madness always at the centre of this?

❖

Chloe: It's a power move, the family not turning up.

Sarah: It's like saying, You are alone on this Earth. You're alone in your supposed innocence. Or you're alone in your guilt. And there is no one apart from your Facebook friend and your lawyers to share the moment. She's thrown to her fate.

Helen: I imagine that's another reason they stayed away—to deny people that moment of spectacle. That is dignity.

Chloe: All Erin's true-crime fantasies have come to fruition in the most horrible way.

Sarah: The jury—I was nervous, but they got there.

Chloe: Imagine them now, having to walk back into their regular lives.

Sarah: Three people died because they relied on good faith that didn't exist. Then she's sitting there for days and days telling us that black is white. In the end, you know, we don't have anything except our word. So, when there's not much to have faith in, the fact that twelve strangers can be plucked from their lives and be told a false story and know in their guts that it's wrong—that's extremely moving.

Helen: It's like after the plane crash we were talking about—you stagger away from it, and you look at the others, the ones who are still alive, and you think, Thank God. And you feel full of love for them.

Sarah: All right, so what will we do now?

CODA

IAN WILKINSON, THE SOLE survivor of the poisoning, addresses Justice Beale in a pre-sentencing hearing. It is 25 August and Erin Patterson is in the dock behind him. He knows how to hold a crowd and his voice rings out in the Supreme Court's high pale room. The sheets of paper in his hand tremble so hard they are flapping. He deplores Erin's crime; he mourns his dear lifelong friends, Don and Gail Patterson; he grieves his wife and praises her strength and sweetness of character. 'I only feel half alive, without her. My consolation is that we will be reunited in the Resurrection and the age to come.' And then he throws out an astonishing challenge, tough and completely without sentimentality: 'I make an offer of forgiveness to Erin. I encourage her to receive my offer of forgiveness for those harms done to me with full confession and repentance. I bear her no ill will. Now I am no longer Erin Patterson's victim, and she has become the victim of my kindness.'

❖

Helicopters circle the Supreme Court. Inside, an enormous chandelier hangs above the crowd as they press and cram into their seats and lean over the public gallery, straining to see. It is 8 September 2025. For the first time in Victoria's history, television cameras have been allowed into the court: Erin Patterson's sentencing is to be broadcast live. There's a hush in the room that's almost like awe.

Here she comes, between her guards, right past where we are sitting. She looks older; her cheeks are thinner and greyer. She takes her seat in the dock and closes her eyes.

Justice Beale appears on millions of screens around the country.

Sombre in black robe and starched white collar, he faces the prisoner and begins to read his judgment.

'Only you know why you committed these crimes,' he says. 'I will not be speculating about that matter. Your crimes, and your pitiless behaviour in remaining silent as your relatives lay dying, fall into the worst category of murder known to the law.'

Erin Patterson does not open her eyes.

'Your lunch guests undoubtedly belong to that company of people among us who do good. The word *senseless*,' he says, 'was repeated in many victim-impact statements, but what also surfaces is hope and gratitude. Simon Patterson gives thanks for the strong, gentle and patient support from everyone around him and his children. He says they have experienced love in a special way since the murders.'

Ian Wilkinson sits in the grand courtroom, watching Erin.

'Mr Wilkinson's offer of forgiveness presents you with an opportunity,' says Beale. 'You would do well to embrace it in the manner he suggests.'

Beale turns to his dilemma in sentencing her.

'Given the unprecedented media coverage of your case, and the books, documentaries and TV series about you, you are likely to remain a notorious prisoner for many years to come. You remain at significant risk from other prisoners.'

In the dock, Erin Patterson now opens her eyes and turns to glare at those in the media rows.

In prison, for her own protection, she is held in isolation. She spends up to twenty-two hours a day alone in her cell. Her meals and medicine are delivered through a flap in the door. She reads, watches television and has taken to crocheting blankets. She can visit the prison library if escorted by two prison officers, but staff shortages make the visits infrequent. Erin's cell has access to a concrete courtyard that measures one and a half by two metres. When granted permission, she can open the door for fresh air. It is also possible, while she is in her courtyard, to communicate through a grille with a woman in an adjacent space. The woman is serving a sentence for acts of terrorism, and has attacked other prisoners. So far, she and Erin have not spoken.

Given these conditions, Beale says, he will set the fifty-year-old a parole date: mercy, a sliver of it.

For each murder, a life sentence. For the attempted murder, twenty-five years.

'All are to be served concurrently. The total effective sentence is life imprisonment.

'I fix a non-parole period of thirty-three years.

'Would you please remove Ms Patterson.'

The camera is switched off.

❖

We hang around afterwards on Lonsdale Street. The strange valedictory feeling, after what we have seen and learnt. A milling about. The need to grasp hands, to touch or hold each other. A deep inner breathlessness, an appalled sorrow. Blind horror of murder, cramped horror of a locked cell. How savage we are, and how fragile. And yet, Ian Wilkinson's offer of kindness—an enlargement of the field.

ACKNOWLEDGMENTS

The authors are grateful to Sarah McVeigh, who recorded many of our conversations with a view to making a podcast. We also wish to thank Cheyne Anderson, Michael Heyward, Jane Pearson, Jane Novak, Tracy Bohan, Andrew Watson, Brenda Niall, Maria Tumarkin, Don Watson, Charlie Pickering, Katya Schiffrin-Sands and Greta Kantor.